Grow, Cook, Dye, Wear

BELLA GONSHOROVITZ

Penguin
Random
House

Senior Project Editor	Krissy Mallett
Project Designer	Vicky Read
Project Editor	Izzy Holton
Senior Designer	Barbara Zuniga
Jacket Designer	Amy Cox
Jacket Coordinator	Lucy Philpott
Senior Production Editor	Tony Phipps
Senior Producer	Stephanie McConnell
Creative Technical Support	Sonia Charbonnier
DTP and Design Coordinator	Heather Blagden
Editorial Manager	Ruth O'Rourke
Design Manager	Marianne Markham
Art Director	Maxine Pedliham
Publishing Director	Katie Cowan
Photographer	Julius Honnor
Illustrator	Geffen Refaeli
Pattern Consultant	Ruta Ramanauskiene

First published in Great Britain in 2022 by
Dorling Kindersley Limited
DK, One Embassy Gardens, 8 Viaduct Gardens,
London, SW11 7BW

The authorised representative in the EEA is
Dorling Kindersley Verlag GmbH. Arnulfstr. 124,
80636 Munich, Germany

For the curious
www.dk.com

This book was made with Forest
Stewardship Council ™ certified
paper—one small step in DK's
commitment to a sustainable future.
For more information go to
www.dk.com/our-green-pledge

For Mr Sadiq

Acknowledgments

I would like to thank the Higham Hill Common
allotment community for teaching me to grow and
nourish. A special thanks to those who wear the
clothes in the book: Mr Sadiq, Paula, Valery and
Ged. To my agent, John Ash and the DK team,
for your dedication. To my collaborators, Julius and
Geffen, for your beautiful contribution and hard
work. To my wonderful family, friends and Philip
for your support and encouragement. To my nephew
Sammy, born as I was writing this book – I cannot
wait to grow, cook and make with you.

With thanks to Charles Shamuraz Smith for the
photograph on page 112.

About the author

Bella Gonshorovitz is a prizewinning fashion designer.
She opened her made-to-measure studio in East
London in 2012, creating fine clothes designed for
longevity. A long-term vegan, her cooking is inspired
by her childhood in Tel Aviv. Growing produce at
her allotment has allowed Bella to experiment with
different crops in the garden and in the kitchen. She
has a clear, engaging vision of how we can live
sustainably and shares this with warmth rather than
worthiness. She lives in Walthamstow, London.

DK would like to thank Amy Slack, Megan Lea,
and Charlotte Beauchamp for editorial assistance.
Glenda Fisher and Eloise Grohs for assistance with
the patterns.

Grow, Cook, Dye, Wear

Contents

Introduction

"The more clearly we can focus our attention on the wonders and realities of the universe about us, the less taste we shall have for destruction," writes Rachel Carson in Silent Spring. Building on this idea, Grow, Cook, Dye, Wear aims to inspire a more sustainable lifestyle. It's a journey from seed to crop, from harvest to plant-based cooking, utilizing food waste to create natural fabric dye for contemporary dressmaking. It explores a joyous process involving five crops: onion, nettle, rhubarb, blackberry and cabbage. In this story they are the lead characters, bringing to life a miniature circular economy. The aim here isn't for you to grow all of your vegetables, hand make all of your clothes, or even convert to a strict vegan die;, it's about establishing a more intimate connection with nature and creativity, and finding a new perspective on mass-produced products. With clothes, as with vegetables, the end product is often presented in a manner detached from its origins and it's too easy to forget that everything we eat, consume and wear comes from nature. This book encapsulates a process rooted in the soil and community that grows around it, and emphasizes the beauty of the journey and how it is reflected in the end result.

The Way I Grow

You temporarily inherit a garden or plot, and for the time it's under your care, your choices shape not only your relationship with it, but also those of the growers that will follow you. When I got my plot in autumn 2018, it was completely overgrown: layers of couch grass and, underneath them, even thicker layers of bindweed and couch grass root systems; clouds of thorny bramble with stubborn roots, which I could barely get to the bottom of. Clearing it took months of daily digging, but it was an incredible education.

I found out quickly, for instance, that my plot used to serve as a nursery for schoolchildren, a place for them to learn about plants. Beneath the thick grass, I found a row of concrete slabs on which the children used to stand. Beneath those, I discovered an abundance of insect life and the most beautiful soil I have ever seen. The tenant who preceded the schoolchildren had a real passion for growing wildflowers, and he had invested a great deal in the soil. I've been told his name was Jackson, a three-time widower. The plot was his sanctuary and he tended it until the very last years of his life.

I knew I wanted to grow organic before I started, but this became the only logical choice once I learnt the plot's poignant history and began to understand the ecosystem already thriving in it. I realized that my work here is not only to grow my own but also to preserve and improve the plot, both for the wildlife and for the next grower. For this reason, I have so far resisted the urge to install raised beds, use shop-purchased topsoil, or use any pesticides. It is impossible to completely tidy the plot, and you constantly need to find creative eco-solutions for slugs or black flies, but you also learn to accept that this piece of land is as much theirs as it is yours.

I allow flowers to self-seed between my vegetables, finding beauty in the eclectic layout and sense in their ability to attract bees and butterflies. As I am still learning (I suspect I always will be), I try to understand why a particular crop will sometimes fail and sometimes thrive. No matter the ratio of success to failure, I always get a diverse and exciting harvest throughout the growing season. And even for someone who is used to creating from scratch – making clothes, cooking, writing – it fills me with immense pride to be self-sufficient in a way that works with, and not against, nature. The joy I get when a seedling I've nursed since early winter finally starts bearing fruit has not yet gone – I hope it never will! It is a magical thing, despite also being the most natural process in the world.

The circular economy of the soil

When I try to explain to anyone how growing things changes your perception of life, I always start with the fact that the most precious commodity for any gardener is horse manure. Huge piles of it are delivered to our site in irregular drops throughout the year, and the moment it arrives a race begins. All the plot owners rush with their wheelbarrows, fill them to capacity, drop them back at their plots, and repeat the process until the smelly, straw-lined matter is completely gone or their muscles fail them. I always find the gold rush for animal faeces humbling. Much like the cooking scraps I add to my compost heap, these horse droppings are usually considered to be the ultimate end of a cycle – waste generated as a by-product of extracting nutrients from food consumed by humans and animals. Not only can we use this "rubbish" to create new plant life, but the fact that it nourishes insects and grows more food is inspiring. It's the best, most natural embodiment of a circular economy, something that's often perceived as an academic and lofty concept – it isn't when you ground it in nature, where nothing ever really goes to waste.

Demystifying and personalizing circularity is one of the key objectives of this book, and for that, there is no better place to start than the soil. I was fortunate with mine – crumbly, dark earth that's incredibly healthy and full of life: worms, woodlice and beautiful caterpillars. I have no doubt that Jackson was a tenacious manure racer, and much of my work is conserving the soil integrity he left me – even such lovely soil has finite resources. As you grow vegetables, they draw their nutrients from the earth, so if you don't replenish them your land will soon be depleted, resulting in a poor harvest and disease. In addition to the rotted manure, I also keep a well-balanced compost heap, fed with food and dye scraps, plucked weeds, cardboard, dried leaves, and even scraps of organic cotton and linen (naturally these take longer to decompose). I also grow nitrogen-rich crops – red clover and alfalfa – which act as "green manure", enriching the land as they wither.

"Nettle tea" is another DIY resource I use. You'll read about this disreputable plant and its often overlooked qualities later (pp64–71). Nettle is seldom a plant one chooses to grow, but this is precisely why it is vital for me to include it (alongside blackberry, which can also be foraged). Having space, and indeed time, to grow things is a luxury: not everyone is lucky enough to have a plot, garden, or terrace. Having access to any of these things mustn't be a requirement for engaging in a meaningful relationship with nature, or the experience packed into this book. Nettle, as a colonizer in areas of human activity, has a way of reminding us that nature is shared between all its co-habitants. Learning to appreciate nettles made me feel closer to the land than any of the crops I have ever cultivated.

How I Cook

*Plant-based cooking makes so much sense when you grow your own —
you really want to taste your produce rather than let meat, butter or
cheese take over. I have been vegan for 12 years, many of them spent
as a closeted vegan. Up until four years ago, it used to be a somewhat
panic-inducing request when attending a dinner party, but we now
widely acknowledge that reducing or completely eliminating consumption
of animal products is (bar boycotting air travel) one of the most effective
things an individual can do to reduce their carbon footprint.*

I keep to a vegan diet because it makes sense for me
and my body. It feels like a natural choice. Still, I don't
believe veganism is for everyone. Instead of trying to
convert people to a strict, plant-based diet, my strategy
is to make vegan food as delicious as possible. I want you
to choose to have a certain dish because you love it,
rather than because it's the moral option.

My style of cooking is very much rooted in my
childhood in Tel Aviv. One of its loveliest, but least

discussed, characteristics is that it's an absolute melting
pot of cultures and cuisines. Take my upbringing as an
example: I'm the daughter of a Polish-Russian father
and a Romanian mother. Growing up, I naturally ate
a lot of borscht and mamaliga, yet some of my most
delicious childhood memories took place in the Arab
hummus restaurant Abu Hassan, in Jaffa, where my
maternal grandparents lived. Another source of
inspiration is my fascination with "veganizing"
dishes encountered in my British adult life. I've
always loved cooking, but growing my own vegetables
has added a new thrill to it. The flavours are different
from shop-bought ones, so I've found myself altering
my recipes or coming up with entirely new ones,
which allow you to really taste the freshness of
your harvest.

Of course, even being fortunate enough to have
a plot, there is no earthly way I could use that piece
of land to grow all the vegetables I cook with during
the year. But growing my own did help me to cook
seasonally and start questioning the origins of produce.
It made me try things I wasn't previously so interested
in, such as jams and relishes, and even cooking tomato
sauce for the purpose of freezing it so that I can enjoy
the flavour of my harvest well into winter.

The Vegan Pantry

"It doesn't taste vegan," is a "compliment" my food often gets.
I take it as such. The tasters often mean that the flavours are
rich and complex, in a way that is harder to achieve without
meat or butter. This requires a spectrum of ingredients that are
more than something I use for an occasional dish, but a live
palette I use to add taste, texture, and nutritional value to
everything I cook. This is how I use them:

Sea salt

Salt is crucial in vegan cooking, as it enhances flavours in a way similar to butter or meat. I use sea salt, mostly in its flake form. It provides a quiet, clean intensity and a freshness that I adore in salads. I also love the smoky version that some brands make, particularly in stews.

Tahini

Tahini goes with everything. Technically classified as a condiment, in the Levant tahini is considered more of a substance: it's as essential and trivial as water. I use this highly nutritious sesame paste in most recipes in this book, including puddings – it's a great binder. Get it from Middle Eastern shops rather than organic retailers.

Date molasses

The Hebrew word for date molasses translates as "date honey" and I consider it an excellent vegan substitution for the nectar made by bees. My usage extends further than that, as I add it to stews, marinades, and bread doughs. Buy or make your own by cooking one part Medjool dates in two parts water for two hours, then strain.

Nutritional yeast flakes

This is a deactivated yeast that is a miracle vegan ingredient. Not only does it add a cheesy aroma to your dish, but it is also a significant source of B-complex vitamins and often fortified with B12, which is low in a vegan diet. I use it as often as I can in soup, pies, stews, doughs, and polenta.

Dukkah

A divine mixture of toasted nuts, sesame, cumin and coriander seeds. Whether you buy it or make your own, always keep a jar to hand to add to your roast potatoes alongside grated nutmeg and herbs. It will add another delicious crunchy element that will lift their crispy edges.

Coconut oil

Coconut oil can replace butter in baking or as a spread, and most vegetable oils when it comes to sautéing onions. I particularly like it in curries and fragrancing a side dish of rice, as its aroma complements the region's spices.

Sea salt, top left; Tahini, top right; Date molasses, bottom left; Nutritial yeast flakes, bottom right.

Pomegranate molasses

I don't use it as widely as its date sibling, but I always keep a bottle in the fridge. It works particularly well in Persian soups or stews – the fruit is native to Persia and considered a spiritual symbol there. It pairs beautifully with rhubarb in savoury dishes, as they both share a flavour profile of tangy sweetness.

Vegan Worcestershire sauce

The original contains anchovies and fish sauce, and is therefore off limits. Luckily, vegan versions are now widely available. A quick and economical way to add that elusive "umami" flavour that can be challenging to create when cooking plant-based.

Vegan stock powder

I like making my own stock and freezing it, but I also don't see any problem in using shop-bought stock, as long as it is of good quality and vegan (do check, as many vegetable stocks are not). I add it sparingly to soups and stews.

Orange blossom water

Distilled from the fragrant blossoms of the orange tree, the flavour of this intensely aromatic water is likely to remind you of baklava. It will add freshness and a mysterious edge to many other puddings, breakfast dishes, and even drinking water.

Ras el hanout spice mix

"Head of the shop" in Arabic, this earthy mixture of cinnamon, cumin, coriander, cardamon, ginger, saffron, and pepper is truly top-shelf stuff. You could make your own, but it's also easy to find in big supermarkets. It's beautiful in marinades, as a coating for roasted vegetables, or rubbed into anything that requires slow cooking.

Aquafaba

Aquafaba is the water drained from chickpeas, whether you cook them yourself or just open a tin. It's my favourite vegan egg replacement, and not just because it's a zero-waste by-product. It's incredible at binding all flan-like puddings and quiches, and even capable of forming impressive meringues.

Khmeli suneli spice mix

My friend Leo introduced me to this Georgian mix, referring to it as "the cheating spice". He was right – it does make any curry, soup, or stew you add it to infinitely better. It's not readily available, but once you get used to cooking with it, you will naturally make sure you keep a good stock of it.

Baharat spice mix

Not a million miles away from ras el hanout, baharat has a distinct peppery flavour provided by the heavy presence of paprika and a touch of chilli. It also contains cloves and nutmeg, giving it a pleasant warmth. I use them interchangeably and quite often together.

Vegan stock powder, top left; Orange blossom water, top right; Vegan Worcestershire sauce, bottom left; Aquafaba, bottom right.

Why I Dye

The most stunning shades in the world are the ones found in nature. This is why, when I started experimenting with dyeing my own fabric, I was quickly drawn to the ancient practice of natural dyes. It also makes sense for a sustainable fashion practitioner. That's a definition I feel confident in embracing, though I battle constantly with the fact that I'm a maker in a world saturated with too many products.

Using natural dye is exciting for many reasons, but the aspect I enjoy most is the unpredictable and experimental nature of the process. There are so many predetermined as well as controllable aspects that will guide the hue I end up with, many of which I discuss below. Very rarely will two dyed lengths end up with the exact same shade – and that, of course, mimics the way colours develop in nature.

Upcycling natural fabrics

As you'll see, I am a big fan of upcycling pre-existing fabric products – bedding, homeware, and even clothes. I love giving these fabrics a new lease of life as freshly made garments, and my absolute favourites are heavy antique French linen sheets, which you can find in abundance online, at car boot sales, and in flea markets. Densely woven and of stunning quality, these kinds of fabric simply cannot be found newlymade nowadays – or certainly not without paying a fortune. They absorb dye beautifully and often benefit from it – as do many old, pre-used textiles that come with imperfections. And the more imperfections, the better the price.

Most of the garments in the book are made from these preloved, all-natural fabrics, as synthetic fibre doesn't bond with the natural dyes. If you come across a textile you would like to upcycle but aren't sure of its content, carefully try and burn a tiny piece of it. Natural fibres burn relatively slowly, their ash smelling like burned paper or feathers. Artificial fibres burn fast, releasing a chemical odour and usually hardening into a bead. Another quick test is crimping the fabric – natural fabrics will crease instantly, while synthetic ones bounce back relatively pristine.

Working with virgin textiles

Upcycled fabrics have already lived a life of use, washed and dried repeatedly. When you get cotton fabric off the roll, it comes straight from the mill. In non-organic fabrics, the manufacturing involves harsh chemicals and heavy metals, on top of the pesticides used in growing the crops. These artificial agents are not just harmful to the planet, they may also damage the natural dye process. Organic cotton is inherently softer and more absorbent and therefore is the optimal choice for a natural dye project, as far as brand new textiles go. As it is relatively untreated, a simple soak with an ecological detergent will prepare it for the binding and mordanting stages. If you are not sure whether or not your fabric is organic (which can happen when you buy dead-stock – surplus material that would otherwise be thrown away), add 1 tbsp of soda crystals for every 100g (3½oz) of fabric to the wash load. This will remove any coating that may act as a barrier to the dye.

Mordanting

A mordant is essentially the dyeing coordinator: it helps establish a link between the colour pigment and the fibre molecules, creating a robust and long-lasting colour. In French, *mordant* means "biting," and I enjoy the idea of the dye "biting" into the fabric. Another common piece of dye jargon is "fast", an adjective used to describe endurance: "washfast" applies to fabric less likely to fade in washes, whereas "lightfast" indicates resistance to change when exposed to sunlight. A good mordant is a critical factor in how "fast" the colour will be.

Alum

Alum is my mordant of choice for the cellulose fibres (linen, cotton and viscose) predominantly used in this book. Commercially available examples of this metallic

salt are aluminium potassium sulphate or aluminium acetate. Used for food preservation, in baking powder, and in some medical creams, alum isn't toxic but needs to be handled with care and never ingested. Alum can be added to the main dye vat itself, but I prefer to mordant separately first, as it can slightly brighten certain delicate shades, particularly pinks.

To mordant with alum, fill a dye vat with water and bring it to a simmer. Carefully dissolve 5g (⅛oz) of alum for every 100g (3½oz) of fabric used into a 200ml (7fl oz/1 scant cup) jar of freshly boiled water. Add the alum solution to the simmering water, stir well, and then submerge your wet fabric or garment. Simmer for one hour while frequently stirring with a wooden spoon, allowing the mordant to interact with every fibre. Leave it to soak for at least four hours or overnight before draining. Rinse and wring the garment, then hang to dry.

Iron

You technically could use iron sulphate in the same way you would use alum, but soaking fabrics in substantial quantities of the solution may weaken the weave. It's better to add it to your main dye vat, where it can act as a (tender) after-mordant and colour shifter. Stir 1 tsp–1 tbsp for every 100g (3½oz) of fabric into your vat before adding the cloth. It'll both increase the wash- and lightfastness and create more sombre, melancholic tones. Iron is an agile agent and there is no need to leave the fabric to soak overnight after simmering, as you would with other mordants or dyes. It may also stain your vat if you don't wash it thoroughly straightaway. You can purchase it as a mint-green powder or make your own iron-infused water by soaking 20–30 rusty nails in a jar that is ⅓ clear vinegar and ⅔ water for two weeks. Both should be handled with care and in well-ventilated environments.

Rhubarb leaves

Rhubarb leaves are a potent natural mordant, one that works particularly well with animal fibres (p124). If I use it to mordant cellulose fibres, I will first bind it with a plant-based milk.

Plant-based milk binding

The prolific natural dyer Rebecca Desnos exclusively uses plant-based milk as a mordant. I get her reasoning. The mordants above are all chemical agents, which aren't dangerous in small amounts, but must be handled

carefully. They're certainly not everyday ingredients like the soya milk she favours. Desnos soaks and dries the fabric repeatedly, to allow the protein to coat the fibre sufficiently. I like to use this method when I need to give a boost of longevity to my dye, whether it's because I'm dyeing an unmordanted fabric with a tannin-rich agent (such as onion skins), preparing vegetable fibre for a rhubarb leaf mordant or iron and dye combination, or before using a more fleeting dye (such as cabbage) and mordanting with alum.

Dilute 1 litre (1¾ pints/4⅓ cups) of your (unsweetened) milk of choice in 5 litres (9 pints/21⅓ cups) of water to submerge 500g (1lb 2oz) of fabric. Leave to steep for 12–24 hours, then wring and hang to dry. I find that one round is enough as a binder but repetition will yield better results.

What else affects longevity?

Time and patience are crucial when it comes to natural dyeing. The longer you can steep your fabric in your dye or mordant, the deeper, more durable colour you will get. I also find that the longer I wait until I first wash my dyed garment, the longer the colour will linger. I always wash my dyed clothes by hand or on a gentle cycle with a mild eco-detergent, avoiding fabric softeners, which compromise the dye.

Preparing your dye vat

Equal weight of dyestuff and fabric is common natural dye wisdom, but this can be misleading regarding tannin-rich ingredients. Onion skins, for instance, can produce intense shades using only 15 paper-thin skins, which can be misleading as they hold virtually no weight. I rarely weigh my dyestuff, other than when I use them for recipes. Whether I work purely with my cooking waste, strengthen my dye vat with more nettles or dried blackberries, or shift the colour by using mixers and modifiers, I find it is best to do it by eye. If I want to check the shade before I add my fabric or garment, I test with a swatch, bearing in mind that a larger piece will always dye paler and that the wet shades will always look stronger (iron the swatch dry for a fast test).

In each chapter, there is a colour spectrum map, with a short description of how to obtain the results. These will send you in a similar direction, but are by no means an exact recipe. The journey of each dye vat is wholly unique.

Modifiers – additives extending the range of shades in your vat

Copper water: Copper sulphate is a great mordant that also provides lovely brown and green hues. I don't use it myself, as it's a toxic substance, dangerous to inhale and an irritant to eyes and skin. Copper water is safer than the crystal form, but I would still use it outdoors or in a well-ventilated room, wearing gloves. To make, follow the iron-infused water instructions, replacing the rusty nails with copper pennies. When ready, the water will turn aqua blue.

pH shifters: These help you change the acidity/basicity level of your dye vat. They can also be used in a separate vat straight after dyeing (p129). Amongst the dyes we explore, onion, rhubarb and cabbage are the most susceptible to pH changes, achieved by using familiar household items such as soda crystals, bicarbonate of soda, and baking powder (alkaline modifiers) and vinegar, cream of tartar, and lemon (acidic modifiers).

Mixers – natural dyes in their own right that introduce new pigments

Madder root: The roots of this lovely plant host an intense red pigment. Obtain it by harvesting your own or buy it as a concentrated powder from dye retailers. Chop the root or add the powder to the vat gradually, a tablespoon at a time.

Woad: Europe's indigo equivalent produces beautiful blues, best triggered with yeast: cover 100g (3½oz) of fresh-cut leaves in boiling water, then steep for 1 hour. Dissolve 1 tbsp of active dried yeast and 2 tbsp of sugar in 200ml (7fl oz/1 scant cup) of hot water. Once the yeast mixture foams, stir 1 tbsp of soda crystals into the steeped leaves, then stir in the yeast water. Heat gently for one hour, then leave to soak until the water turns blue before using.

Oak galls: Incredibly rich in tannins, oak galls, like rhubarb leaves, are a powerful natural mordant. Collect them from the back of the leaves as they shed on the ground in autumn and add to the dye vat to obtain grey and brown shades. A little goes a long way.

Chlorophyllin: This is the green pigment that plants use in photosynthesis. It can be purchased as a dietary supplement or from dye retailers in powder form. 1 tbsp is enough to invigorate any green vat.

Black tea and coffee grounds: Use the ones you have already brewed to muddy colours. Add gradually for the desired shade.

To dye before or after?

You could dye your fabric before you sew or after the garment is ready. Dyeing the fabric length before you cut the pattern will give you more control: natural dyes rarely give continuous, even cover. Pre-dyeing allows you to choose the best patches of colour for each part of your garment, but also means you might need more dyestuff (or to dye only a few lengths of fabric at a time, as dyeing more than 1.5m/5ft lengths in a single vat usually leads to patchy results). Dyeing a made garment is easier, but you mustn't forget that fabric can shrink in high temperatures. This is less of an issue in the main fabric used in this book, as antique French linen would have been washed at high temperatures throughout its lifespan. If in doubt, pre-shrink the cloth in hot water before you start sewing. Always use a cotton thread for a garment you are planning to dye or re-dye (p26).

Dyeing domestically

I always separate my cooking gear from my dyeing equipment – it's certainly necessary if you use alum or iron as mordants. Of course, you may choose to dye only with plant-based milk as a binder, in which case you'll have no issues with using your all-purpose stockpot as your main dye container, also known as the dye vat. Still, if you really get into the dyeing habit, you'll find that your pots and wooden spoons will colour over time – perhaps not something you want to risk with your primary kitchenware. But there's no need to purchase a brand-new saucepan. I always try to approach sourcing my equipment in the same way I source fabric by repurposing old items, quite often worn-out ones. A big advantage with dye equipment is that it need not be immaculate – you can use a rusty pan that someone left out in the street during a house clearance (rust acts like iron mordant and will yield darker shades), a worn-out Teflon pot no longer safe for cooking, or a charity-shop find. My dye gear contains all of the above, but my two most reliable dye vats are second-hand cauldrons sourced, like many of my favourite objects, cheaply online. As well as being beautiful, with their antique aesthetic, their best property is being made out of aluminium which encourages a more vivid dye, as, with sustained heat, it will shed alum.

As for disposing of the dye-vat water, there are no issues with pouring the liquid into a ceramic sink – as long as you give it a good clean straight away. Think about it as the same as chopping cabbage – if you don't wash your chopping board promptly, it's likely to remain stained. The same goes for your dyeing gear, particularly if you use iron mordant, which tends to stain pots quickly. In environmental terms, if you do a lot of alum mordant-based dyeing, you might want to consider saving the liquid between dyes, as alum does contain metal which we should avoid adding in large quantities to the water system. Dye vats that contain purely vegetable-based water can be used for watering plants. Some plants that thrive in acidic soil, such as blueberries or hydrangeas, would even benefit from some alum-induced water. Water them with the leftovers of your mordant vat.

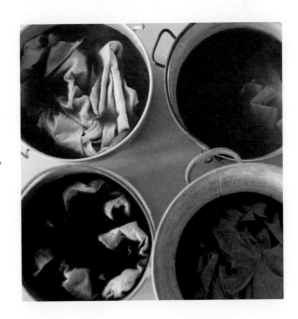

What I Wear

My friends and family often comment that I've worn the same clothes for many years. It's not as if I'm devoid of the need for novelty, but I find that I have a strong relationship with my clothes that begins when I'm designing or making them. To me, clothes become imbued with memories of sights, scents, and people. That connection between clothes and life was one of the main reasons I decided to become a fashion designer. It's why I treat my clothes as friends, accepting the imperfections they develop and mending them where possible.

The growing phenomenon of sending clothes to landfills baffles me – I find the idea of throwing my beloved garments in a bin genuinely upsetting. So even if there is a piece of clothing that doesn't fit me any more, I try and find it a new home with a friend. I love seeing my garments being worn by someone else and always hope that the piece will become suffused with memories for them, too.

I spent a few years studying the link between fashion and psychology, learning about the idea that we come to embody the garments we wear and that they influence the way we think, feel, and function. Perhaps there's a link between this phenomenon and the desire to buy new clothes – they carry a promise of who we may become while wearing them. In that context, this book attempts something radical: the clothes that emerge from this book say more about the past, represented in the making process, than the fantasy of the future. In other words, it is about who you became on the journey.

It's why I called the last stage of the process "Wear" rather than "Sew". The lifespan of clothes can, and should, be long, and the making part is just a short time in a garment's life – yet it lingers, creating a meaningful relationship with the wearer based on a shared experience.

Sew easy

I know that sewing can be daunting, but really, it is not that different from gardening, or even cooking. Imperfections can be beautiful, and practice will lead to better results.

Many of the sewing hacks I am going to share in this book have come from ex-Soviet seamstresses I worked with over the years – the most skilled, resourceful, and disciplined professionals I know. But the best sewing tip came from the very talented Tatiana, originally from Tajikistan, and had nothing to do with technical stuff. "You need to really love the craft of sewing, savour every moment of it, relish the sound of the machine, the heat of the iron, the feeling of the cloth in your hands." It was such a simple, yet profound, observation and it changed the way I approach creative practices.

All too often we get competitive about our makes, or demand too much of ourselves. So whatever level you are, make sure you enjoy it. Allow enough time and space for it and approach stages methodically, never skipping a good press with a hot iron. "In Russian, we have this phrase – the iron will fix whatever the machine messed up." That's another thing Tatiana said, though her machine never really seemed to fail her. Perhaps because it was guided with so much love.

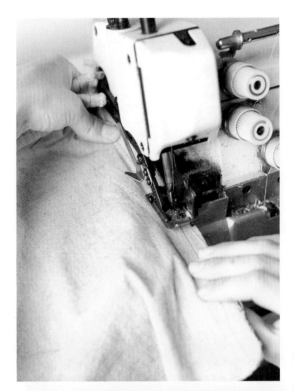

The Patterns

Sizes

I hate clothing sizes – there is no regulated standard, and even if there were, the fluctuating nature of our bodies could often make us feel confused and upset as we move between them. I'm not alone – most fashion professionals I meet hate them, too. When I was working at threeASFOUR, the avant-garde label in New York, they tried to omit sizing altogether and classify the garments under the names of their lead designers: Gabi, Adi, and Ange. It was a novel idea, but unless you knew them personally, you wouldn't be able to tell which size you'd require.

Despite my resentment, the patterns in this book are classified according to "traditional" (ish) womenswear sizes – even though most of the relaxed-fit styles are gender-neutral. The Nettle Duster and Blackberry Shirt(dress) have been graded in the widest range (6–8 to 22–24), so they can accommodate broader shoulders or a more petite frame. The Onion Dress is what you might almost call a one-size garment, spanning the range of 8–24 in four size grades – it's the drawstring gathering that allows it to be so versatile and comfortable. The most "fitted" garment in the book, the Rhubarb Bolero, still leaves enough room to manoeuvre for a grade jump of 8–10 to 20–22, with its romantic, yet practical, bow-tie fastening. The only garment graded in single jumps (8–22) is the Cabbage Shorts, as trousers of any kind are always the hardest to fit, particularly as gender-less pieces.

You may require different sizes for different styles: the best way to work it out is to take your measurements for each piece and compare them to the range detailed in the size tables in the relevant appendix (pp218–223). Follow the advice in each chapter to help you achieve your unique fit.

Using the patterns

Tracing

To keep this book accessible, the pattern sheets are printed doublesided, which requires copying. The best way to use them is to pin dot-and-cross paper (p27), or another lightweight paper, to the sheets. Using a ruler

and a curve tool, start with the straight grain, then move to the outline of your relevant size, following the numbers marked in the pattern corners. Trace carefully, using a sharp pencil, paying attention to notches, pocket, and button marks and fold lines.

There is no need to add seam allowances – they are all included within the patterns (and will be indicated in the sewing instructions).

Cutting

Maintaining the straight grain is key to getting a good drape and fit. This is more obvious in shop-bought fabric, where the grain runs parallel to the selvedge (the tightly woven edge), but it can be tricky in upcycled textiles. You will still find it running along the long edge of many of the antique French linens and tablecloths, or concealed underneath a double folded "hem". If you are repurposing a ready-made garment, unpick it and snip along the longer edge of the fabric. Rip downwards to discover the grain. As you pin the pattern to the fabric, measure an equal distance from both ends of the straight grain to your fabric edge (see image opposite). Cut as close as you can to the edge of the pattern with sharp fabric scissors, snip 5mm (¼in) into the seam allowance to mark notches, and thread-mark pocket placements. Take time to do this right: press your fabric beforehand (particularly if you have pre-dyed it) and work as precisely as you can. It will make the sewing part a lot more pleasurable, and your garment will hang and wear better.

My sewing arsenal

Measuring tape

My most sturdy tape measure is about the same age as my set square. It never breaks or splits. It's essential in maintaining a straight grain when I cut the pattern (always measure the distance between the marked grain line of the pattern and the salvaged edge of the fabric, maintaining an equal space at the top and bottom).

Cotton thread

This is more expensive than a polyester thread but will take natural dye, unlike polyester. The larger cones are more economical; I always keep one in off-white handy.

Interfacing

I always use knitted interfacing, as it tends to last longer. I recently used new, recycled woven interfacing with good results, but it's too recent to know how it will behave after years of wear.

Set square

I'd never encourage you to buy anything from plastic unless you'll use it for life. My set square is 17 years old and I'd be lost without it. It helps me mark straight lines and straight angles up to 15cm (6in), and draw bias lines. I don't even mind that I broke the corner about a decade ago.

Pins

These are crucial, particularly as you are building confidence. Always look out for long, thin ones as short, heavy ones may cause holes and break your machine's needle.

Dot-and-cross paper

Dot-and-cross paper is great for tracing patterns, as it's thin enough and you can pin the dot and cross on the grainline, making sure you are keeping things straight as you go along.

Worn-down soap bar

This is my favourite equipment hack. Use it as you would tailor's chalk. It will fade away with steam and also smell lovely.

Improvized pattern weights

Use large stones as pattern weights when you are tracing and cutting, to keep everything in place.

Scissors

Good-quality fabric scissors are for life. Keep them sharp and never use them to cut anything else.

Card for pressing

I keep these hanging by the sewing machine to press crisp hems, pockets, and anything that needs a strong fold line.

Onion

I didn't plan to grow onions when I started my vegetable garden. It was a decision taken for me by the man who came to be my growing mentor. Mr Sadiq always had a way of rewarding me for clearing another patch in the overgrown plot I inherited, which had once belonged to his late friend. The back left of my plot, cleared in late January, was planted with bright primrose in my absence. The following month, he repaired the wooden handle of a digging fork that had snapped as I battled thick couch-grass roots. And on the evening of the first of April, I found two modest rows of onions (a mixture of brown and white varieties). Initially I was slightly cross – I had other plans for that area of the plot. But I knew I wouldn't dare pull out Mr Sadiq's onions, and not merely because they were a gift. After all, one of the first things I had been told about him was that his onions "are legendary". So I looked after them with gratitude, but I only fell in love as I harvested them – they were truly extraordinary, and not just because everything you grow yourself tastes extraordinary. Since then, I have devoted a sizable patch to growing my own.

Sow Onion

Mr Sadiq starts his onions from seed. I know he would disapprove, but I like growing onions from sets (adorable-looking baby onions, offered for sale in early spring). They are straightforward to start off and less prone to disease. Sets are heat-treated during the winter and so are less likely to bolt, which is precisely why Mr Sadiq doesn't like them. He has a habit of leaving a few plants of each of his crops to bolt and flower prematurely. It's quite a beautiful sight but it comes at a price, as part of the harvest is sacrificed. For him, however, it is a worthy transaction...

The seeds Mr Sadiq rips from the flowers of his bolted vegetables allow him to preserve the varieties he brought over from his native Pakistan. Like many traditional growers, Mr Sadiq also favours seeds because they are more economical and yield larger bulbs – the size that wins him the "best onion" award at the association summer show every year.

So as well as planting sets, I also start a tray of Mr Sadiq's seeds every winter – mainly for the excitement of having something to sow in the early days of the new year. You can sow the seeds close together. Onions started from seeds, endearingly, savour each other's company and happily grow in clumps. Despite the fact they can look pretty meagre compared with other young seedlings, they are a ravenous bunch and require good-quality, free-draining potting compost.

Like many seeds, they need heat to germinate. I keep them moist in a heated propagator, but any warm room will do. As soon as they germinate, I move them to a west-facing windowsill to soak up as much light as the short winter days can offer, as onions need plenty of sunshine to thrive. I transplant them alongside the first sets in late March when day and night (nearly) reach an equal length – my own spring equinox celebration.

Onions perform well even in soil of relatively unremarkable quality, as long as the soil has good drainage and is moisture retentive. In fact, soil that has been freshly enriched with manure can encourage bulb rot. If you'd like to improve your soil before planting, it's best to do so weeks in advance, letting the organic matter disintegrate properly. If you're lucky enough to have rich soil to start with, pair the onions with lettuces, which will relish the nitrogen boost. Another good growing mate is parsley, which keeps the onion fly away.

I rotate my growing bed through the seasons to protect the soil quality. I know there is an enormous debate in the gardening community on whether this long-established practice is necessary, but it really is with onions and others in the allium family – garlic, leeks, and chives. These edible alliums are highly prone to fungal diseases and pests (such as white rot and eelworms), which can persist in the soil for years. It is good practice to plant onions after umbellifers, such as celery, carrots, and coriander. These aromatic flowering vegetables can reduce build-up in the soil of certain fungi alliums are affected by.

As big a fan as I am of eclectic bed layouts, I like to plant my seedlings and sets in traditional rows, as they are easier to care for. I allow 30cm (12in) between each row. I usually keep one row of seedlings, transplanting them to the growing bed in clumps of up to six, spacing them 30cm (12in) apart. I thin them through the growing season and as they mature I enjoy them as spring onions. I dedicate the rest of the bed to sets, knowing that whatever the seasons have in store for us, or whatever diseases may spread on site, they are more likely to grow reliably and rapidly, even if they do not produce the biggest bulbs.

While I keep the seedlings 30cm (12in) apart, it is enough to keep 15cm (6in) between each miniature set bulb. Conveniently, this is roughly the distance between my thumb and my stretched index finger. I simply push my fingers into the ground and place them in, the pointy tip just visible once covered with soil. Birds often mistake these tips for worms, giddily pulling them out of the ground. You may prevent this by protecting them with a securely fastened net, but I like to place recently pruned tree branches between the rows. It's another hack I learnt from Mr Sadiq.

Varieties

I like to have a good mix of colour in my onion bed:
White: As an everyday kitchen staple, I like reliable, strong, high-yielding varieties: "Setton" produces slightly darker, straw-coloured bulbs; "Sturon" produces medium-sized, sharp-flavoured bulbs; and "Hercules", which produce larger bulbs, store well over winter.
Red: I love the pop of bright colour these bulbs add to the soil. My favourite is the popular "Red Baron", which I have cultivated successfully from both sets and seeds. They have a stunning blood-red hue and pungent flavour. For something more adventurous, I go for "Long Red Florence", which produces elongated bulbs with a mild and sweet flavour – lovely in salads or for pickling.
Misc: I adore French market pink varieties such as "Rose de Roscoff", "Isobel Rose", and "Pink Panther", which all produce rosy, sweet and juicy onions that taste like summer to me.
I have recently taken to overwintering onions, which are planted in early autumn for an early summer harvest. Hardy as nails, the Japanese "Senshyu Yellow" variety is the most reliable I have come across to date.

Cultivate *Onion*

Mr Sadiq once gave me an invaluable piece of advice: onions and garlic can't stand tap water. This wasn't something I'd come across in any gardening manual, but I never doubt Mr Sadiq. Born in Pakistan in 1933, he received his plot in 1984 – the year I was born – so he knows this soil as well as I know myself. Still, to prove it, on that early summer day he suggested a little experiment. For the rest of the season, I was to water only half of my onions and garlic with tap water, even when the other half looked a little parched. He was right, of course...

By harvest time, the "neglected" half of the crop had caught up, their bulbs larger and healthier than the ones I had tended regularly with my watering can. Knowing when and when not to water your onion crop can be a tricky balance to strike, especially as we are experiencing more extreme weather patterns. As I am writing this chapter, we are in the midst of an early summer dry spell, following an unusually cold spring that started in a month-long drought and ended with weeks of heavy, almost tropical-like downpours. My onions – and even Mr Sadiq's – are suffering.

In arid periods, it is best to give the bulbs a good soak once a week, rather than watering little and often. Of course, too much water over a long period can also be pernicious. It can result in mildew, which can be detected by looking out for brownish or powdery stains on the onion leaves. Removing affected leaves may save the plant, but the bulbs may not store for long.

Another recent yet widely spread pest is the allium leaf miner fly, whose presence can be identified by spotty white stains or deformed curly leaves. If you suspect your onions have been attacked, it is best to dig a couple of bulbs out and look for the tiny brown pupae, usually embedded in the lower stems or bulbs. Once the crop has been affected, little can be done and

sadly, it must all be pulled out. It is best to burn the infected plants – take them to be burnt in an industrial composter at your local composting facility or recycling centre. Adding them to your compost heap is likely to breed a second generation attack.

Prevention is the best course of action. Covering young seedlings securely with fine net or mesh at the peak of egg-laying season, from March to April and from October to November, may help deter miner flies and will also protect the crop from onion fly.

In a year of acute weather patterns, which can disturb the equilibrium of conditions required for healthy growth, I like to plant a second, early summer round of sets in May or even early June. These late onions are unlikely to reach the size of their earlier peers, but they would still get nearly 100 days of growth. These late sets and the onions I grow in large pots in my garden are my fallback plan in case the earlier crop fails, which happens – even to the most seasoned growers.

Weeding

Later in the summer, the top foliage channels energy into the bulbs, helping them swell. In the build-up to this stage, they rely on incredibly long roots to reach deep into the soil and pull up water and nutrients. To eliminate competition on these precious resources, it is essential to weed the onion bed religiously, particularly in the first half of the growing season. I use a short hoe between rows but pull the weeds individually by hand between the bulbs, as its sharp edge may damage them.

Harvest *Onion*

Onions will let you know when they are ready to be harvested. It can happen seemingly overnight, though there are signs to look out for: the edges of their leaves start to brown and you can tell that the bulbs, having nearly pushed themselves to the top of the soil, have reached a sufficient size. But the final stage, when the foliage spontaneously collapses, always catches me by surprise, usually on a late summer evening. I'm always enchanted by my first encounter with these beings I have cultivated for so long – their colour, smell, and the texture of their skin...

When harvested, the onion skins will be still be fresh with moisture. For the skins to develop their familiar papery character, onions require drying – although I can never quite resist taking a couple home the same night I pull them to enjoy fresh in a summery salad. Drying ensures that your onions will store well, perhaps even through the winter if they are kept in a cool and dry place. If particularly dry weather is forecast, I leave mine on the plot to dry in the sun for a minimum of three days. I use a raised wire mesh I got from Mr Sadiq – it allows for all-round air circulation, much like leaving a freshly baked loaf of bread on a cooling rack. If rain is on the horizon, I take the onions home and hang them over the washing line whenever the sun comes out, sometimes even alongside some freshly dyed fabric. This makes for an eccentric display, much to the amusement of my neighbours.

Every summer, as I pull my onions out of the soil, I think about how at odds this act is with modern-day living. At the supermarket I could easily buy a whole bag of perfectly nice, perhaps even organic, onions with the loose change in my pocket. Onions, usually the starting point rather than the star of a dish, are not a particularly popular "grow your own" crop for precisely this reason. Unlike heirloom tomatoes or "Crown Prince" squash, they are far from prized vegetables. But as far as I know, there are no onions I could buy that would taste as good as the ones I grow. I savour *my* onions and use them for salads or dishes in which I can really taste their astringent yet sweet flavour. I enjoy their vibrant colour – both on the plate or as it soaks into cloth when I add onion skins to a dye vat.

....

Small Spaces

Onions ask for the basics that a vegetable needs to thrive: plenty of direct sunlight and rainwater. Annoyingly, lack of exposure to either of the two will lead them to fail, so they will not grow well in shaded gardens or on sheltered terraces. However, they will do well in pots on exposed balconies or roof terraces or even in large window boxes – as long as they get a minimum of six hours of sun and the container is at least 15cm (6in) deep to accommodate their long, stringy roots. Spacing between sets can be tightened, but this will affect bulb size (p33). Onions can also be planted in unorthodox layouts in a garden. One of my favourite plots on the site, known as "Mr Onion's plot", uses onions as border decoration around small trees and shrubs.

....

Slow Roasted Onions

Serves 4 as a side or as a part of a mezze platter

Onions were worshipped by the Ancient Egyptians as symbols of eternal life. Their spherical shape and perpetual layers, they believed, encapsulated an eternal existence. They even buried the dead with onion bulbs and adorned gravesites with allium flowers. I know this might not be the most appetizing onion anecdote, but what I love about it, and this dish, is that it makes you realize how miraculous onions are. The beauty of the ring within a ring pattern, the harmonic structure, is a design that could only be created by nature. This dish is so simple (waiting for the onions to soak in the marinade is most of the work here), but incredibly impactful. It's the kind of side that my guests often respond to as though it was the main dish.

Ingredients

6 onions, any variety, peeled (save the skins for dyeing)
75ml/2½fl oz/⅓ cup olive oil
2 tbsp balsamic vinegar
1 tbsp soy sauce
2 tbsp date molasses
1 tbsp picked thyme leaves
sprinkle of chilli flakes
1½ tsp sea salt flakes, plus extra for sprinkling
3 sprigs of rosemary, each cut into 2 pieces
freshly ground black pepper

Method

01 Trim the top and bottom of each onion, then cut them in half horizontally.

02 Place the onions, cut side down, in a 30cm/12in round or 20cm/8in square roasting tin.

03 Combine the oil, vinegar, soy sauce, molasses, thyme, chilli flakes, and salt in a measuring jug and then season with pepper.

04 Pour the mixture over the onions and leave them to marinate, covered, in a cool place for at least 1 hour and up to 12.

05 Flip the onions over so that the wider, well-marinated, sides are face up. Leave to marinate for another 1–4 hours, preheating the oven to 200°C/180°C fan/400°F/Gas 6 about 15 minutes before the end of the marinating time.

06 Flip the onions over again and top each one with a sprig of rosemary and a sprinkle of salt.

07 Roast, uncovered, for 45 minutes or until the centres are golden and the edges caramelized – recoat the onions a couple of times with the marinade as they cook. Serve hot or at room temperature.

Onion, Purslane, Herb, and Sumac Salad

Serves 4

This is the salad I make when I naughtily pick a couple of onions just before they are ready to harvest and rush home to taste them fresh. It features one of my other late-season favourites, purslane. Purslane is, technically, a weed. It is indeed very invasive, but I intentionally introduce it to my plot and I'm delighted when it spreads around. Not only does it have a wonderfully unusual, succulent, texture and an irresistible salty-sour flavour, it is also naturally rich in omega-3 (containing more than any other leafy green vegetable) and packed with antioxidants. I urge you to try and grow it (it's incredibly easy) and incorporate it into your diet, particularly if you are vegan. If it is out of season, or you cannot get a hold of it, increasing the herb ratio in this salad will keep it deliciously crisp.

Ingredients

2 red onions, peeled (save the skins for dyeing)
splash of balsamic vinegar (optional)
85g/3oz purslane or a mix of the herbs below
40g/1½oz parsley
25g/1oz mint leaves
20g/¾oz dill
10g/¼oz tarragon
12 cherry tomatoes, halved or quarted
30g/1oz pumpkin seeds, toasted

For the dressing
3 tbsp olive oil
2 tbsp lemon juice
1 tsp sumac
1 tsp sea salt flakes
freshly ground black pepper

Method

01 Cut the onions in half and then into thin slices.
If their taste is too astringent for you, soak them in
cold water (with a splash of balsamic vinegar) for
around 15–30 minutes.

02 Chop the purslane and herbs. I like my herbs roughly
cut, even torn by hand, but it is a very personal choice.
I wouldn't, however, chop the purslane too finely.
Keep it proportionate to the onion slices.

03 Combine the (drained) onions, purslane, herbs and
tomatoes in a large bowl.

04 Whisk the dressing ingredients together in a bowl until
thoroughly combined, then pour over the salad and mix
well. Sprinkle with pumpkin seeds and serve.

Onion Buns

Makes 12–14

When I first made these buns for my friend Rosie, she said they made her nostalgic, yet she was unsure about exactly what or why. We had very different upbringings, but I feel the same. The buns are related to cebulaki, Polish onion bread rolls, yet this recipe carries more of the flavours from my Romanian mum's side of the family. They remind me particularly of the baked goods my grandfather treated us with. Taking a trip to the Abouelafia Bakery (a local institution and a symbol of coexistence between Jews and Arabs) and trying all kinds of oriental pastries from there was the highlight of visiting my grandparents in Jaffa. Abouelafia's buns were covered in za'atar, whereas these are topped with poppy seeds – a touch of the Eastern European seasoning my grandparents cooked with at home.

Ingredients

330g/11½ oz/2⅔ cups strong white flour, plus extra for dusting
170g/6oz/1⅓ cups strong wholemeal flour
1 tbsp dried active yeast
1 tbsp poppy seeds, plus extra for sprinkling
1 tbsp sea salt flakes, plus extra for sprinkling
3 tbsp date molasses
5 tbsp olive oil, plus extra for greasing
3 onions, any variety or a mix, peeled and chopped
  (save the skins for dyeing)
zest of 1 lemon
4 tbsp aquafaba (the liquid from a tin of chickpeas)
  or plant-based milk

42

Method

01 Combine the flours, yeast, poppy seeds, and salt in a large mixing bowl. Add the molasses and 3 tablespoons of the oil and start to combine the mixture while gradually adding 250ml/8¾fl oz/ generous 1 cup water. I like mixing the dough with my hands, but you could also use the bread attachment of a food processor.

02 Dust your work surface lightly with flour. Tip the prepared dough out of the bowl and knead by hand for 5 minutes. Alternatively, mix on medium speed for 5 minutes in a food processor.

03 Place in a well-greased bowl and cover with a damp tea towel. Leave to rise for 2 hours or until the dough has nearly doubled in size.

04 While the dough is resting, prepare the onion topping. Heat 2 tablespoons of oil in a large frying pan and sauté the onions over a medium heat until they are soft and beginning to brown. Add the lemon zest, mix well, and leave to cool.

Once the dough is ready, divide it into 12–14 equal-sized balls. Form each ball of dough into a rough disc about 7cm/2¾in in diameter, but don't flatten them. Transfer to a large baking tray lined with baking paper – leave a little space between them, as they will spread when baking.

Using your knuckles or the back of a spoon, make a well in the centre of each disc. Divide the onions equally between the buns, pressing them in with your fingers. Brush the tops with aquafaba to give the crust a handsome brown finish. Allow the buns to rest for 10–15 minutes while you preheat the oven to 185°C/165°C fan/365°F/Gas 4½.

05 Sprinkle the buns with poppy seeds and sea salt flakes. Bake the buns for 25–35 minutes until the tops and bottoms are golden brown. If the buns are not browning evenly, you can rotate the baking tray halfway through baking.

06 Transfer the buns to a wire rack and allow to cool for 10 minutes, before serving. The buns can be kept in a dry, airtight container, stored in a cool place, for up to three days. Freeze for up to a month.

Stuffed Onions

Serves 4 as a side or as a part of a mezze platter

When we think of onions, it is primarily their pungent taste and smell that come to mind. Their inherent sweetness is understandably overlooked – after all, sweetness is something we mostly associate with desserts and the idea of incorporating onions in one is frankly cloying. This dish highlights their sweet quality while keeping them strictly in starter, main or mezze platter territory. Although the onions are the stars of this dish both on the palate and on the plate – with their endearing shell-like structures – the stuffing holds its own. You can replace the wheatberries with bulgur wheat, which is a little easier to come across, but I encourage you to find the former. Wheatberries have a lovely nutty flavour and a chewy texture that works so well with the silky consistency the onion layers develop when cooked.

Ingredients

100g/3½oz/heaped ½ cup wheatberries or bulgur wheat

4 large onions, any variety or a mix, peeled (save the skins for dyeing)

70g/2½oz/½ cup dried apricots

30g/1oz mint leaves

20g/¾oz parsley, plus extra to serve

2 garlic cloves, peeled

3 tbsp olive oil, plus extra for drizzling

30g/1oz pine nuts, toasted

½ tsp chilli flakes

1 lime, zest ½ and then juice

½ tsp sea salt, plus extra to season

½ can chopped tomatoes (200g/7oz)

2 tbsp date molasses

freshly ground black pepper

Method

01 Put the wheatberries in a medium pan and cover with plenty of cold water. Add a pinch of salt, bring to the boil, then reduce the heat to low and simmer for 45–55 minutes (or 20–25 minutes for bulgur wheat) until the grains have a tender, slightly chewy texture. Drain and allow to cool.

02 Trim the ends of the onions. Carefully make an incision on one side of each of the onions, cutting only as far as the centre from top to root. Cook in a pan of boiling water for 10 minutes or until the layers soften and separate easily. Drain and leave to cool.

03 Chop the apricots and herbs. (Don't chop them too finely – keep them proportionate to the pine nuts.)

04 When the onions are cool enough to handle, carefully peel and set aside their outer layers. You will need 16–18 layers, or "shells", in total. You can use the outer,

thinner layers and the middle, chunkier ones – as long as they are large and sturdy enough to hold the filling.

05 Chop the leftover onions with the garlic. Heat 1 tablespoon of the oil in a frying pan and sauté the onions and garlic for 7 minutes, stirring frequently. Remove from the heat and leave to cool.

06 In a large bowl, mix the wheatberries, apricots, herbs, onion and garlic mix, pine nuts, chilli, lime zest and juice, salt, and the remaining oil. Season with pepper.

07 Preheat the oven to 200°C/180°C fan/400°F/Gas 6. Place one tablespoon of the filling in the centre of each onion shell, wrapping the sides of the shell tightly around the filling. Arrange the filled shells on a large baking tray and drizzle with a little olive oil.

08 In a measuring jug, mix together 100ml/3½fl oz/ scant ½ cup water, the tomatoes and date molasses.

09 Drizzle a third of the tomato sauce over the onion shells and roast for 30 minutes or until golden brown, drizzling another third of the sauce over the onions every 10 minutes or so. Serve warm, sprinkled with chopped parsley.

Grandmother Bella's Salad

Serves 4

Pickling is an age-old harvest preserving practice, one that growers used to be dependent on when things were genuinely seasonal. These aren't the pickles that will take you through the winter, but the kind you could keep in the fridge for a month. I like to use them in salads and particularly in my twist on the Olivier Salad. My father tells me that my grandmother, Bella, who I was named after, was a spectacular and resourceful cook. Sadly, as she died 15 years before I was born and didn't leave a recipe book behind, I never got to try her food. This is how I imagine she would have adapted this traditional salad of her native Russia with the flavours of the new Middle Eastern land she arrived at in the sixties – had she been vegan. The potatoes are roasted with spices rather than boiled, the carrot is replaced by fresh cucumber, and the mayo-like dressing benefits from a touch of tahini.

Ingredients

For the pickled onions

90ml/3fl oz/½ cup unfiltered apple cider vinegar

2 tbsp date molasses

1 tsp sea salt

2 red onions, peeled and sliced (save the skins for dyeing)

2 garlic cloves, peeled and sliced

½ red chilli

½ tsp mixed peppercorns

3 bay leaves

½ tsp dried oregano

2 star anise

2 sprigs of dill, finely chopped

For the salad

6 medium potatoes, unpeeled, washed and chopped into wedges

2 tbsp olive oil

1 tsp dukkah

1 large or 2 small cucumbers, cut into 2-cm/¾-in chunks

150g/5½oz/1 cup fresh peas, cooked

2 tbsp capers

20g/¾oz dill, chopped, plus extra to serve

freshly ground black pepper

For the dressing

75g/2¾oz silken tofu, drained

3 tbsp olive oil

2 tbsp tahini

2 tbsp lemon juice

1 tsp sea salt flakes, plus extra for seasoning

freshly ground black pepper

Method

01 For the pickled onions, heat the vinegar, molasses, and salt in a saucepan over a medium heat, stirring until the salt dissolves. Allow to cool, then pour over the onions. Add the rest of the ingredients and stir well. Cover and refrigerate for at least 2 hours, or until the onions have turned bright pink.

02 Put the potatos in a pan and cover with water. Bring to a rapid boil and cook for 7 minutes. Meanwhile, preheat the oven to 200°C/180°C fan/400°F/Gas 6.

03 Drain the potatoes and transfer to a baking tray. Drizzle with the oil, sprinkle with dukkah, and season with salt and pepper. Mix with a spoon to get an even coating and gently press the potatoes as you go so they are ever so slightly smashed. Roast for 20–30 minutes until they are crispy on the outside. Leave to cool to room temperature.

04 Using a hand blender or a whisk, mix the ingredients for the dressing until smooth. Season with pepper.

05 In a large bowl, mix the cucumber with the cooled wedges, pickled onions, peas, capers and dill. Add the dressing and mix to combine. Serve at room temperature, or cooled, sprinkled with dill.

Dye with *Onion*

In 2014, I interviewed esteemed trend forecaster Lidewij Edelkoort for *Time Out* magazine. I think of her as an anthropologist who identifies trends as long-term, meaningful changes to social undercurrents. Back then, sustainability wasn't a term associated with fashion; in fact, I'm not sure she even used it herself in that interview. But Lidewij was alarmed about the state of an industry that adopted a model of mindless growth: the exploitation that fuels fast fashion was epitomized by the Rana Plaza disaster that had occurred nine months earlier. She also believed in change and that a future generation would oppose the broken system. "That generation's colour will be yellow, much like pink defined the Millennials," she said. Yellow, she explained, is the colour of the sun nd the sand. It can be intense and serene, the colour of reckoning and light. I think of that yellow, the reckoning yellow, when I dye with onions.

Yellow shades

You can use many other dye plants to achieve different yellows, but onions produce some of the most beautiful and complex shades. It is a quality of yellow that comes across as both poised and fervent. My favourite onion dye combines brown and red skins – I often don't even bother to separate them from any leftover flesh connected to their tips if I use them fresh. I cover the onion skins with water in a cauldron, bring them to a boil, and then simmer for an hour. I don't even strain the skins before I add the fabric – they make the dye strike in uneven patches, sometimes leaving spots of green or purple pigment. I embrace the serendipity.

Often, rather than dyeing my fabric before cutting out the pieces for the Onion Dress (which would allow me to select which areas of the fabric I want to use for each piece), I add a finished dress to the dye vat instead.

I stir well with a spatula to make sure the dress is submerged and to remove air bubbles, and leave it in the vat overnight, or for up to 48 hours, for maximum saturation.

The varied results yielded by this method are exactly what I pictured for the Onion Dress. For years, it's been my summer wardrobe staple. The one I wear when I want to feel comfortable when I work in my studio, attend the plot, or cook. Consequently, my dresses are washed frequently, and even though mordanting increases their washfast durability, I might dye them a couple more times as the season progresses. Sometimes I redye a dress to restore the vitality of the colour – even synthetic dyes tend to lose their vibrancy if they are washed frequently and dried in the sun. Sometimes I redye a dress to modify it, making it a few shades stronger or changing its colour altogether.

....

Collecting and storing skins for dye

To dye a finished Onion Dress, you will need about 15–40 onion skins, depending on how strong you want the colour to be. I can easily reach the lower threshold in several days, particularly if I am hosting a dinner party, in which case I just keep all my onion waste in a covered bowl in the fridge and tip it all into the dye vat. If you are collecting onions for a longer period of time, separate their papery skin from any remaining flesh and keep it in a cool, dry place in a paper bag or open container – they need to breathe, otherwise they'll go mouldy. You can keep using the same skins for a few consecutive dye vats, as long as your dyeing sessions are scheduled close together so the skins don't go off or become too gooey. Once that happens, compost them.

....

Earthy hues

Fabric dyed yellow in an onion dye vat can be redyed to achieve a range of earthy hues. A bright orange shade can be achieved by adding madder root (or madder powder) to the dye vat with the onion skins. Shades of rust and brown can be obtained by adding iron mordant gradually into the vat until the desired hue is achieved (you could test this with a small swatch of fabric, but do remember that the greater the volume of cloth, the weaker the shade will be, and that the cloth always dries a shade lighter). I love this "dye over dye" solution, as it is a way to satisfy that novelty craving for a new garment we often get when the weather changes in a way that requires little effort or resources. In that respect, it feels revolutionary, although it is an ancient practice used to invigorate stained garments or ones that have aged with time.

Pinks

You can also start your Onion Dress journey in pink. Dyeing with red onion skins only will yield heartening shades of seashell pinks. Pre-mordant your fabric with alum or bind with plant-based milk in a separate vat before you dye (pp20–21), as the presence of alum in the dye vat may disturb this delicate colour. Of course, you may choose not to mordant or bind the fabric. Onions contain tannin, an organic compound that can be used as a natural mordant, which means that the colour of your onion-dyed fabric will last for longer than other natural dyes would on their own. Some dyers rely on the tannin to act as the colour fixer but if, like me, you plan to wear your dress a lot, I'd encourage you not to skip the mordanting stage. If you'd like to cut steps and are happy with a dirty mauve colour, you could add an iron mordant solution to the dye vat. Increasing the amount of iron in the solution will progress the shade of your fabric to a rosy tan.

Greens

Onions are inherently acidic and sometimes can give shades of green, which can turn into a mustard or a light olive or khaki colour. It depends on the pH level of the water, something that is difficult to foresee or manage unless you measure it. If you want to induce that reaction, add 1–2 tbsp white vinegar to the dye vat for every 100g (3½oz) of fabric.

I used this dye for my "fancy" Onion Dress (see right image). This dress was made of a beautiful antique linen, which I purchased online. Significant areas were spotless enough to cut the back and front pieces of the dress. Others were stained and worn and had to be cut away. I dyed the leftover pieces and cut the pockets, hem facing, drawstring and channels from them. I like how this is a way to "hack" a pattern using dye only, as it feels so radically different from my other dresses. I love how my onions transformed this stunning, yet severely damaged piece of fabric, perhaps an old tablecloth in its previous life, into a joyfully chic garment.

See pages 18–23 for more detailed information on techniques, dyestuff, mordants, and dye vat ratios.

Upcycling fabrics

I encourage you to work with preloved textiles for all the garments in this book to complete the circular economy idea at its heart. The Onion Dress, in particular, is wonderfully impressive when cut from old French linen sheets. Their weight lends itself beautifully to the shape of the dress. Another advantage of working with such fabric, which has been washed and dried for about a century, is that you don't need to do much more than dampen it with warm water before you start to dye it. Try to use pure linen – it's the most sustainable and airy fabric, and its unique drape works best with this cut.

Onion colour range

The weight of the Onion Dress is typically 250–500g (9oz–1lb 2oz), depending on the fabric used. These tentative dye "recipes" are for 100g (3½oz) of fabric – multiply the quantities as required and use enough water to cover the fabric. Bear in mind that the shade may vary depending on your fabric, water pH level, the array of shades of onion skin, and serendipity.

Olive

Medium-weight coarse French linen, mordanted with alum. Dyed with the strained skins of 12 brown and yellow onions and ½ tbsp white vinegar for every 100g (3½oz) of fabric. Boiled and simmered for 2 hours, steeped for 4½ hours.

Yellow

Medium-weight coarse antique linen. Dyed with the unstrained skins of 8 yellow and brown onions for every 100g (3½oz) of fabric. Boiled and simmered for 1 hour, left to steep for 2 hours. Natural onion tannins employed as a mordant. Patches of the fabric left randomly unsubmerged.

Mustard

Lightweight French linen tablecloth, mordanted with alum. Dyed with the strained skins of 10 yellow and brown onions for every 100g (3½oz) of fabric. Boiled and simmered for 2 hours, steeped for 4 hours.

Pink

Medium-weight antique linen. Dyed with the strained skins of 10 red onions for every 100g (3½oz) of fabric. Boiled and simmered for 1 hour, steeped for 4 hours. Natural onion tannins employed as a mordant.

Orange

Medium-weight French linen, mordanted with alum. Dyed in an aluminium vat with the strained skins of 12 red onions and 1 tbsp of iron water and ½ tsp of madder root powder for every 100g (3½oz) of fabric. Boiled and simmered for 1 hour, steeped for 4 hours.

Rust

Medium-weight French linen. Dyed with the strained skins of 7 red onions and 5 brown and yellow onions and 1 tbsp of iron sulphate powder for every 100g (3½oz) of fabric. Boiled and simmered for 2 hours, steeped for 4 hours.

Tan

Medium-weight French linen. Dyed with the strained skins of 12 red onions, 1 tbsp of iron-infused water, and 1 used tea bag for every 100g (3½oz) of fabric. Boiled and simmered for 2 hours, steeped for 5 hours.

The Onion Dress

For me, the Onion Dress is the epitome of summer. It is free and effortless, yet grand in its movement and vibrancy. It is the perfect dress for hot days when you want to feel like you aren't wearing anything yet know you are clad in something beautiful and unique. What I love most about this dress is the negative space between the fabric and the body. It feels like it just lets you be. It looks good with a t-shirt underneath or even an oversized cardigan on top. It is truly a morning-to evening-dress, one that I cannot wait to live my life in as soon as the weather gets hot.

Construction

Shown on the right are the pattern pieces for the Onion Dress (please see Pattern Sheet 2).

Dress, drawstring channel and facing: the front and back are cut from the same pattern piece – the centre back fold line is 3cm (1³⁄₁₆in) in from the front. Once you've cut the front pieces, fold the pattern along the centre back line before positioning on your fabric.

On the front and back pieces, cut down the fold from the neckline to the opening mark.

All seam allowances are 1cm (³⁄₈in) unless otherwise stated.

Measurements

Please refer to the appendix on p218 for size charts and fabric requirements. As this is the most loose-fitting garment in the book, determine your size according to your bust measurement.

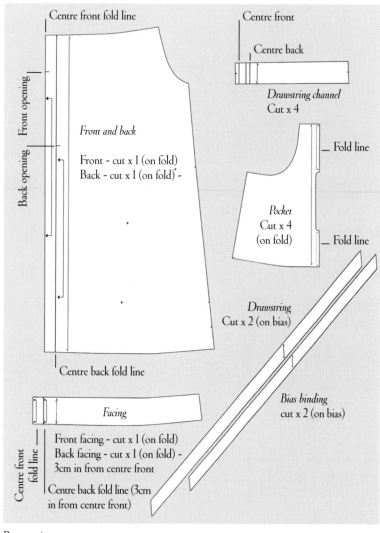

Pattern pieces

Method

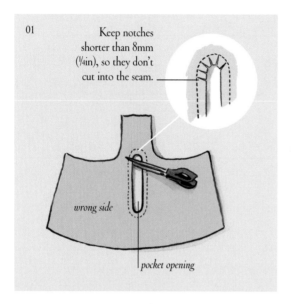

01   Keep notches shorter than 8mm (¼in), so they don't cut into the seam.

wrong side

pocket opening

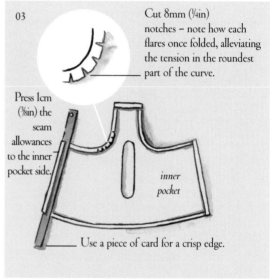

03   Cut 8mm (¼in) notches – note how each flares once folded, alleviating the tension in the roundest part of the curve.

Press 1cm (⅜in) the seam allowances to the inner pocket side.

inner pocket

Use a piece of card for a crisp edge.

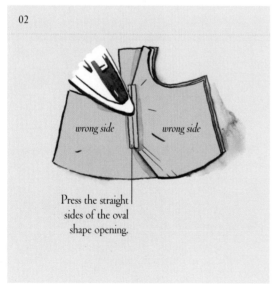

02

wrong side   *wrong side*

Press the straight sides of the oval shape opening.

01 **Prepare the pockets**

Each pocket is constructed from two layers of fabric to strengthen the openings. Pin the two layers right sides together, pinning around the oval cut-out. Stitch around the cut-out. Cut notches in the curved part of the seam allowance.

02 "Bag out" by pushing one layer of fabric through the cut-out section and flipping the sides of the pocket back so that the two layers are facing right side out. Then flip each side of the pocket back in turn and press the straight sides of the cut-out open. Lay both layers flat and press the pocket flat. Choose which side will be visible from the front (the outer pocket) and which side will line the inside of the pocket (the inner pocket).

03 With the inner pocket facing up, stitch around the outside edge of the pocket to secure both layers together. Cut 8mm (¼in) notches in the roundest parts of the curves. Press the seam allowances over to the inner pocket side, using the stitch line as a guide. Start with the curves, then the top edge, bottom edge and sides. Repeat steps 1–3 to prepare the other pocket.

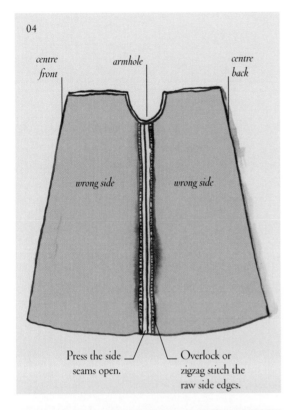

04

centre front · armhole · centre back

wrong side

wrong side

Press the side seams open.

Overlock or zigzag stitch the raw side edges.

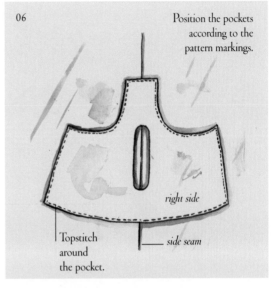

06

Position the pockets according to the pattern markings.

right side

Topstitch around the pocket.

side seam

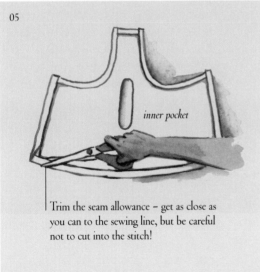

05

inner pocket

Trim the seam allowance – get as close as you can to the sewing line, but be careful not to cut into the stitch!

04 **Join the front and back pieces**

Overlock or zigzag stitch the raw side edges of the front and back pieces. (Make sure you feed the fabric through the machine with the right side facing up.) Pin the front and back right sides together and sew the side seams. Press the side seams open and turn the dress right side out.

05 **Attach the pockets to the dress**

If your fabric is quite heavy, such as antique French linen, it may help to trim the seam allowances of your pockets before attaching them to the dress. I find that snipping the seam allowance of just one layer down to 2mm (1/16in) sufficiently reduces the bulk while leaving enough grip to sew the pocket properly.

06 Pin the pockets to the dress according to the pattern markings. Topstitch around the outside edge of the pocket in one continuous line, positioning the inside edge of your sewing machine foot on the very edge of the pocket and using it as a guide to help you maintain a neat, straight stitch line.

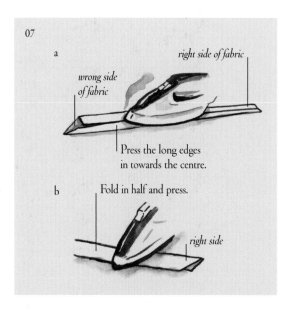

07

a

*wrong side
of fabric*

right side of fabric

Press the long edges
in towards the centre.

b

Fold in half and press.

right side

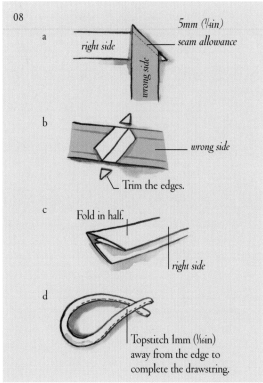

08

a

right side

5mm (¼in)
— *seam allowance*

wrong side

b

wrong side

Trim the edges.

c

Fold in half.

right side

d

Topstitch 1mm (¹⁄₁₆in)
away from the edge to
complete the drawstring.

07 Prepare the bias binding for the armholes and front and back openings

Take your bias binding fabric strips and press the long raw edges in towards the centre by 5mm (¼in) – (a). Fold in half and press again, taking care not to stretch the fabric (b).

08 Prepare the drawstring

The drawstring will help you adjust the fit of your dress and also forms the straps. Unlike the binding for the armholes and front and back openings, the drawstring requires just one long piece. You may need to join two fabric strips together to achieve the required length. To do this, pin the strips right sides together at a 90-degree angle (a). Stitch together, taking a 5mm (¼in) seam allowance. Press the seam open and trim the edges (b).

Take the drawstring fabric strip and press the long raw edges in towards the centre by 5mm (¼in). Fold in half and press again, taking care not to stretch the fabric (c). Press the short edges in by 5mm (¼in) in as well. Topstitch around the three open sides of the drawstring in one continuous line, sewing 1mm (¹⁄₁₆in) from the edge (d), pivoting at the corners.

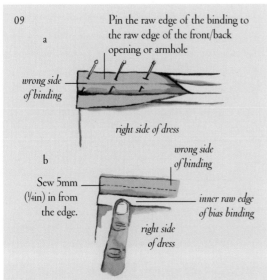

09
a

Pin the raw edge of the binding to the raw edge of the front/back opening or armhole

wrong side of binding

right side of dress

b

wrong side of binding

Sew 5mm (¼in) in from the edge.

inner raw edge of bias binding

right side of dress

10
a

inner raw edge of bias binding

stitched binding edge

b

right side of binding

c

Sew along the folded edge.

wrong side

d

armhole

Stitch and press the binding so that it's concealed inside the dress.

wrong side

09 Bind the armholes and front and back openings

Open out the first strip of bias binding. With right sides together, pin it to the raw edge of the front opening, aligning the edges (a). Sew along the pressed line in the binding (b), then trim off the excess.

10 Fold the binding over the opening (a) to the wrong side of the dress (b). Fold the binding to the wrong side of the dress again, so that it isn't visible from the right side. Sew along the folded edge to secure it in place (c). Press. Repeat steps 9 and 10 to bind the back opening and the armholes (d).

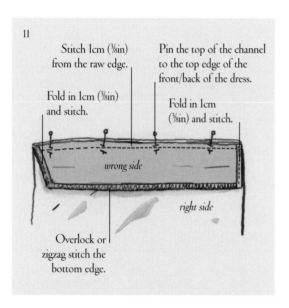

11

Stitch 1cm (⅜in) from the raw edge.

Pin the top of the channel to the top edge of the front/back of the dress.

Fold in 1cm (⅜in) and stitch.

Fold in 1cm (⅜in) and stitch.

wrong side

right side

Overlock or zigzag stitch the bottom edge.

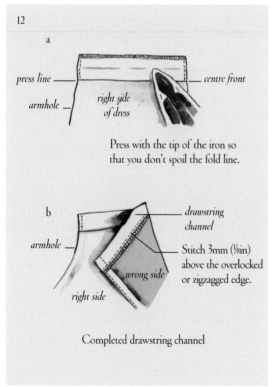

12

a

press line

centre front

armhole

right side of dress

Press with the tip of the iron so that you don't spoil the fold line.

b

drawstring channel

armhole

Stitch 3mm (⅛in) above the overlocked or zigzagged edge.

wrong side

right side

Completed drawstring channel

11 Attach the drawstring channels

There are four drawstring channels in total – one for each side of the front and one for each side of the back. To prepare each one, overlock or zigzag stitch the bottom raw edge. Fold the short ends to the wrong side by 1cm (⅜in), then press and stitch in place 1mm (1/16in) from the raw edge. Press the channel in half, longer edges together and right sides facing out. Open the channel out flat. With right sides together, pin the raw edge to the top edge of the dress and stitch in place.

12 Flip the channel up and press the seam flat (a). Fold the channel over to the wrong side of the dress along the line pressed in step 11. Press and pin in place. Stitch the channel in place 3mm (⅛in) above the overlocked or zigzagged edge (it may be helpful to draw this line with an erasable pen). Repeat steps 11 and 12 to attach the remaining drawstring channels.

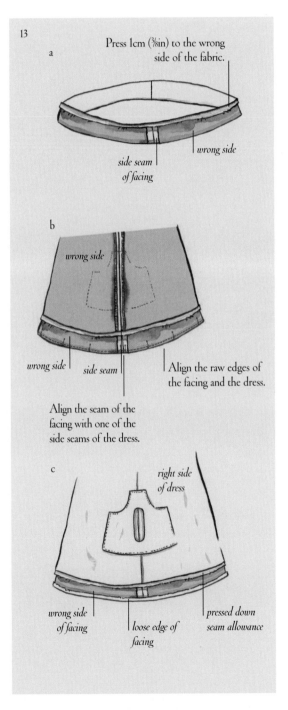

13

a

Press 1cm (⅜in) to the wrong side of the fabric.

side seam
of facing

wrong side

b

wrong side

wrong side   side seam   Align the raw edges of
the facing and the dress.

Align the seam of the
facing with one of the
side seams of the dress.

c

right side
of dress

wrong side
of facing   loose edge of
facing   pressed down
seam allowance

13 Attach the facing

This is a separate pattern piece used to finish the hem of the dress and will be visible on the right side of the garment. Pin and stitch the front and back facings right sides together 1cm (⅜in) along one short edge. Press the seam open. Repeat with the other short edges (note that the front and back facings are different lengths). Stitch around the top edge of the facing. Fold the facing to the wrong side, using the stitch guide and press (a).

Turn the dress inside out. With the right side of the facing against the wrong side of the dress, matching the seams of the facing to the dress's side seams and aligning the raw edges, pin the facing to the hem. Sew in place 1cm (⅜in) (b).

Press the seam allowance towards the bottom of the facing. Press the long raw edge of the seam 1cm (⅜in) towards the wrong side of the fabric.

Turn the dress right side out (c) and press the seam allowance down.

NOTE: The facing is hanging loose at the bottom, which allows us to flip it up and stitch it in place in step 14.

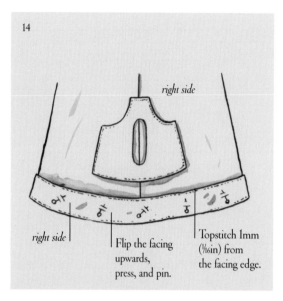

14

right side

right side | Flip the facing upwards, press, and pin. | Topstitch 1mm (⅟₁₆in) from the facing edge.

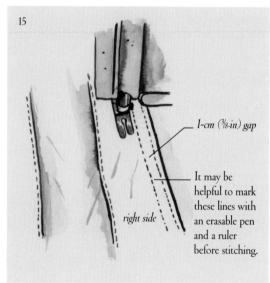

15

1-cm (³⁄₈-in) gap

It may be helpful to mark these lines with an erasable pen and a ruler before stitching.

right side

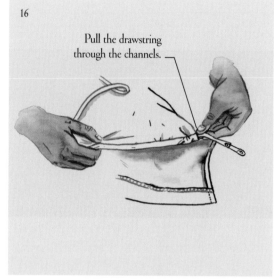

16

Pull the drawstring through the channels.

14 Flip the hem facing up along the previous stitch line and press. Pin the loose edge of the facing to the right side of the dress. Topstitch all around 1mm (⅟₁₆in) away from the edge, using the inside edge of your machine foot as a guide. Press.

15 Add 5 decorative lines of stitches to the facing, 1cm (³⁄₈in) apart. Press.

16 **Insert the drawstring**

Attach a safety pin to the end of the drawstring and use it to help you pull the string through the channels. Tie the drawstring in a big loose bow at the front or back, according to your preference.

NOTE: To determine the length of your straps, try the dress on. I like my Onion Dress intensely gathered with 18-cm (7-in) straps, which keeps a snug fit on the bust, but I let them go a bit longer when I feel like having a more open décolleté.

Nettle

When I talk about nettles, I am talking about stinging nettles (well, mainly). They can be found on riverbanks, towpaths, and moorlands, as well as in woods, marshes, and gardens. They also thrive in edgelands where you often spot abandoned ruins like old cars. The plants reclaim the space for nature, as ladybirds devour the aphids sheltering amongst them and caterpillars, butterflies, and moths relish them as a food source, as do seed-eating birds come autumn. Yet nettle isn't chiefly known as a wildlife sanctuary. It's the infamous sting that precedes its reputation. You probably remember your first encounter with it — I certainly do. In fact, it's one of my earliest childhood memories. I grew suspicious of all leaves after that, and it took me a while to rebuild my confidence. I thought about that fearful little girl when I bounced with joy the day I noticed nettle had self-seeded itself in my plot, for as an adult, I know what a miraculous plant it can be: it's packed with nitrogen and minerals that are beneficial to your plants; it's a delicious, nutrient-rich, versatile leafy green that's steadily emerging as an unlikely superfood hero; it can be used to create sustainable textiles, and of course, it provides a rich source of natural dye. You can forage it for free and free of concern — as long as you wear a good pair of protective gloves!

Appreciate *Nettle*

When I started researching nettles, I quickly gathered that I could have written a whole book just about the different types. The nettle family, Urticaceae, currently consists of more than 2,600 species: herbs, shrubs, small trees, and even a few vines. Most of them are tropical plants, but a few, those native to Europe, North Africa, and most of Asia, can be found growing in abundance worldwide. Here's a quick guide to the qualities and characteristics of three types that can be found in the UK and USA and are perfect for the recipes and natural dyes suggested in this book...

Common stinging nettle (*Urtica dioica*)

Common stinging nettle grows nearly everywhere in a half-mile radius from my front door: in the unkempt patch of land at the end of my road, in the local parks and marshes, and even between the bricks of the railway arches at the nearest train station! Indeed, common nettle is incredibly invasive and grows in dense clonal patches. It spreads through both creeping rhizomes (underground stems) and seeds – each shoot can produce up to 20,000!

If you don't keep common nettle in check, it will take over your growing beds. As its season starts earlier than almost any other plant, it is wise to use it as an early crop, harvest its tender leaves, and then pull it after it attracts the aphids from other crops but well before it goes to seed. You can use it as a perennial mulch around fruit plants and trees, as its high potassium content aids their production, or add it to the compost heap. You can also make a natural "fermented tea" fertilizer by submerging it in a covered bucket of water for a couple of weeks. It will smell awful once you strain it, but your nitrogen-loving plants – particularly rhubarb – will revel in it.

Dwarf nettle (also known as annual nettle, *Urtica urens*)

This is the type of nettle that self-seeded in my plot last year. The first thing I learnt about it – the hard way – is that its sting is more potent than that of the common stinging nettle. The second, much more pleasant observation I made is that small tortoiseshell butterflies, excellent garden pollinators, love it and as such the nettle provides much-needed breeding grounds for declining butterfly populations.

As its name suggests, it is much smaller than the common nettle, about a third of its height. It doesn't tend to grow in such dense clumps as its taller relative and often mixes with other weeds. As it is more scattered and smaller in size, it is harder to harvest or forage significant amounts. I tend to mix it with my common nettles, particularly when I dye, as its brighter leaves add a boost of chlorophyll to the dye vat. Its culinary uses are akin to those of the common nettle.

Dead-nettle (*Lamium*)

Dead-nettle isn't a nettle, really – it belongs to the Lamiaceae family and is biologically closer to mint and sage than to any *Urtica* genus. It was named after the common stinger as they share quite a lot of physical characteristics. Researchers believe the cause for this was evolutionary – that adopting the appearance of their distant relatives afforded similar protection from predators, tricking them into assuming they possess the same powerful venom. The truth is, dead-nettles don't sting at all. Their leaves have a slightly velvety and actually quite pleasant texture. They're generally smaller than the dwarf nettle, and their long-flowering blooms are an important source of nectar and pollen for bees in the milder winter months. As there is no need to blanch them to remove the skin, their young leaves can also be eaten raw in salads, which allows you to get even more of their nutrients. They provide excellent ground cover in gardens, but as they tend to grow in swathes in the wild, you can still enjoy them in abundance even if your growing space is limited.

Forage *Nettle*

*I like to think of nettle foraging as the common rite of early spring.
It's a time when not much else is ready to harvest, or even plant
outdoors, which makes their lush-green, tender new shoots so appealing.
I once read that the optimal time to pick them is right in the middle of
February, and I like the irony of handling a plant that stings you as
you get close to Valentine's Day. You can get away with just scissors
for protection at this early stage, as it's always better to clip the leaves
rather than pull them, to encourage plant rejuvenation...*

If you're foraging for common nettles later than mid-February, glove up and wear long sleeves. As the plants grow, their stems and leaf bottoms get progressively covered in the hairs responsible for their distinctive sting. These hypodermic needles evolved to protect the plants from animals that might want to eat or uproot them, and they are savage. Even a casual rub unleashes a brew of neurotransmitters, histamines, and formic acid – also present in the agonizing bee sting. If, like me, you sometimes get too enthusiastic (or nonchalant) about nettle picking and do get stung, neighbouring plants might offer some relief. Although they're sometimes dismissed as a placebo, I find that the large leaves of the dock plant can be crushed and rubbed against the skin and even form bandages; the sap found in jewelweed stems, which favours the same growing condition as nettle, is another natural remedy.

As to what part of the plant you should pick, the rule of thumb is to focus on the top leaves. I mostly follow this time-honoured wisdom, but I find that when the shoots are young enough, the whole plant is edible, including the tender stems. You can find these in abundance in February, but new growth occurs all the way to mid-summer – although you may need to observe the ground for longer to discover fresh ones. Older plants with tougher and more fibrous leaves are still edible, as long as the plant is no higher than 45cm (18in). In terms of the recipes in this book, older leaves will be more suitable to the

How to recognize

Common nettle – the common nettle is quite distinct: it grows in clumps up to 1.8m (6ft) in height; the strongly serrated leaf margin, with a slightly cordate base and a sharp tip, are strong characteristics; and you'll see the delicate, troublemaking hairs on the wiry stems and the leaves. If you're still in doubt, a light touch will confirm you are dealing with the stinger. But I would deploy it as a very last resort!
Dwarf nettle – although their culinary and herbal uses are interchangeable, their appearance is distinct from their common sibling. At the outset, they are much smaller, 40cm (16in) on average. Their leaves are much brighter (and primarily darker), with more defined serrated edges.
Dead-nettle – its characteristics immediately divulge the fact it is part of the mint plant family: the square stems, undivided leaves, and double lipped flowers, which come in white or purple. The leaves are fuzzy to touch and don't sting.

nettle soup than the pesto, as they will benefit from a longer cooking time. That said, avoid foraging the leaves of plants that have flowered or gone to seed. In that late stage, the foliage contains oxalate, which can irritate the kidneys.

But bolted nettles are far from useless – you can still use them to strengthen your dye vat, adding them to the blanching water reserved from the edible leaves. What's more, they provide some of the most nutritious, easily obtainable wild seeds, traditionally used to alleviate stress and burn-out fatigue. You can eat them straight from the plant – they don't sting! Just remember, nettles are monoecious plants and the seeds of the female flowers contain all the nutritional benefits (although the male ones won't harm you). As they tend to grow side by side, take a bit of time to identify them: female seeds are heavier and sometimes appear "frostier" than their male counterparts. If you aren't sure, observe the plants for a while – in full sun, the male plants' flowers will release pollen into the air. You won't catch this in a glimpse; you really have to sit down and look for these subtle movements. It may feel like a rather demanding engagement, certainly for a plant that is so common that we hardly ever reward it with a second glance, but it is a lovely way to spend a balmy, late-summer afternoon within nature.

Given its edible bounty and practical uses, it is interesting thinking about nettle as the pest it is often considered to be in the garden. Don't get me wrong – I completely understand why it developed such a bad reputation, even if you put the stinging aspect aside. But it can inadvertently look after your other crops, too – it's a good indicator of soil frailty, particularly low calcium levels, which can cause stunted growth and make plants more susceptible to pests and diseases.

Wild food to superfood

Along with many other edible flowers and weeds, common nettle featured heavily in recipes that preceded the Industrial Revolution. Local and readily available made sense until it didn't, and the demand for more "sophisticated" food rose. It's interesting to reflect on this as we adapt our food consumption habits in response to the climate crisis. Take me, for example: up until a few years ago, I mostly enjoyed nettle in

(biodegradable) tea bags rather than as something I foraged and cooked with regularly.

This changed during a visit to my dear friend Leonie in North Italy. The nicest dinner I had on that trip was a risotto she cooked with nettle leaves we foraged on the hills in the rural outskirts of Turin. Leo grew up in these hills in Rivalba, a relatively isolated village, and I think that is why she is one of the most creative and practical people I know. For her, nature is a source of inspiration, nourishment, and substance. As she blanched the nettles to remove their sting, she sang their praises: anti-inflammatory, detoxifying, full of iron, vitamin C, potassium, calcium, beta-carotene, and surprisingly rich in protein.

These remarkable qualities underpin the fairly swift transition common nettle has made in recent years – from wild food to superfood. It features in plenty of supplements, tonics, skincare products, and tea infusions (which I still enjoy, only now I brew my own). Still, when I first learnt you could buy nettles in many urban farmers' markets, I was a bit baffled: as a plant that grows in most ecosystems and is so readily available, I found it hard to believe anyone would be happy to pay for it. But in some big metropolises, nettle is not so prolific or grows on sites that could be contaminated with heavy metals, making it unsuitable for consumption. Some also avoid foraging for it in trepidation: of the sting (though they sting you no less if you buy them packaged) and of mistaking it for another, inedible plant.

Foraged or market purchased, nettles make me hopeful. Consuming them is an act of resourcefulness, connecting to nature in a way that may seem trivial but makes so much sense. It's a gateway to incorporating more local, readily available "weeds" in our lives and diets, a reminder that forward-looking sustainability practices are often at their most ingenious when we observe forgotten traditions from the past.

Nettle Chraime

Serves 4

I very rarely, if ever, crave non-vegan food; especially not in recent years, when vegan versions of pretty much any type of food you can imagine have been widely available. There is only one dish that makes me miss my pescatarian days – chraime. It literally means "hot" in Arabic, and it is indeed a very spicy fish and tomato Libyan stew. I have been trying to veganize it for years and this is my most successful attempt to date. The key here is blanching the nettle leaves in very salty water that tastes like the sea. This, alongside the seaweed, gives an ocean aroma to the patties. The tomato sauce is as hearty as in the non-vegan version and is particularly comforting when mopped up with a slice of freshly cut bread.

Ingredients

For the patties
1 tbsp + 1 tsp sea salt flakes
150g/5½oz nettle leaves
300g/10oz silken tofu
30g/1oz breadcrumbs
15g/½oz dried, shredded seaweed
3½ tbsp olive oil
4 garlic cloves, peeled and finely chopped
30g/1oz coriander, chopped
1 tbsp nutritional yeast
1 tsp ground cumin
1 tsp ground cinnamon
1 tsp ground ginger
juice of ½ lemon
3 tbsp raw tahini

For the tomato sauce
3½ tbsp olive oil
2 onions, peeled and chopped (save the skins for dyeing, p48)
8 garlic cloves, peeled and finely chopped
1 green chilli, finely chopped
1 red pepper, deseeded and diced
2 tbsp sweet paprika
1 tsp ground cumin
1 can chopped tomatoes (400g/14oz), or 400g/14oz fresh tomatoes, chopped
2 tbsp date molasses
juice of ½ lemon
50g/1¾oz coriander leaves, chopped
2 tsp sea salt flakes
freshly ground black pepper

For the hot green pepper paste
2 green peppers, deseeded and diced
1 green chilli
juice of ½ lemon
¼ tsp sea salt flakes
½ tsp nutritional yeast
4 tsp olive oil

To serve
raw tahini
chopped parsley or coriander leaves
sourdough or vegan challah bread

Method

01 First make the patties. Bring 2 litres/3½ pints/8½ cups water with 1 tablespoon of the salt to the boil in a large saucepan. Using gloves, carefully add the nettles and blanch for 3 minutes. Remove using a slotted spoon or tongs (save the blanching water for the nettle dye, p82), then plunge the nettles into a bowl of cold water. Once cool, drain and pat dry with a tea towel.

02 Preheat the oven to 200°C/180°C fan/400°F/Gas 6 and line a large baking tray with greaseproof paper. In a large bowl, combine the blanched nettles with the remaining ingredients for the patties. Mix well (the batter shouldn't be too smooth). Scoop out a ping-pong-size ball of the mixture, flatten it into a pattie, and transfer to the lined tray. Repeat with the remaining mixture. You should have about a dozen patties. Bake for 15–20 minutes until firm and golden.

03 To prepare the sauce, heat the oil in a medium saucepan over a medium-high heat. Lower the heat, add the onions, and cook for 5–7 minutes until translucent. Stir in the garlic and cook for another minute. Stir in the chilli, pepper, and spices and cook for 5 minutes. Add the tomatoes, molasses, lemon juice, coriander, and salt. Season with pepper and cook for another 5 minutes. Add 1 litre/1¾ pints/4⅓ cups freshly boiled water and cook for 20 minutes over a medium-high heat, uncovered. Lower the heat, add the baked patties and cook for 10 minutes.

04 Meanwhile, make the pepper paste. Combine all the ingredients in a pestle and mortar or food processor (I prefer the former, as it helps release the natural oils of the ingredients and makes for a lovely serving dish).

05 Serve the chraime hot, topped with pepper paste, tahini, and parsley or coriander, with some sliced bread for dipping.

Nettle Spanakopita

Serves 4

Spanakopita is all about the (traditional) combination of spinach and feta cheese, so this is quite a departure. But it works. The key to getting it right is not to be too cautious with the salt – feta cheese has a real salty punch to it, and although I love the vegan "cheese" used here (and eat it quite happily spread on bread or baked as a cheese ball), there is no point in pretending it's the same. And being different isn't a bad thing. My Greek friend Sophia said that any Greek mama would approve of this version of their national pie. This was such a compliment – particularly as Sophia isn't vegan and is the kind of person who would never shy away from expressing her honest opinion, no matter how blunt.

Ingredients

For the vegan "cheese"
100g/3½oz/¾ cup cashew nuts, soaked in freshly boiled water for 1 hour and drained
1 garlic clove, peeled
1 tbsp raw tahini
1 tbsp olive oil
2 tbsp nutritional yeast
juice of ½ lemon
1 tbsp sea salt flakes
1 tsp za'atar (optional)
freshly ground black pepper

For the filling
300g/10oz nettle leaves and tender stalks
1 tsp sea salt flakes
2 tbsp olive oil
1 onion, peeled and chopped (save the skin for dyeing)
3 garlic cloves, peeled and finely chopped
6 spring onions, finely chopped
20g /¾oz dill, finely chopped
20g/¾oz parsley, finely chopped

To assemble
4 tbsp olive oil
10 sheets filo pastry
1 tsp nigella seeds

Method

01 To prepare the nettles for the filling mixture, bring
    2 litres/3½ pints/8½ cups water with the salt to the boil
    in a large saucepan. Using gloves, carefully add the nettles
    and blanch for 3 minutes. Remove using a slotted spoon
    or tongs (save the blanching water for the nettle dye,
    p82), then plunge the nettles into a bowl of cold water.
    Once cool, drain and pat dry with a tea towel.

02 Put all the "cheese" ingredients in a food processor
    (or use a hand-held blender). Season with black pepper
    and combine until a thick, crumbly paste forms.

03 For the filling, heat the oil in a large frying pan over a
    medium-high heat. Lower the heat and add the onions.
    Cook for 7 minutes, then add the garlic and cook for
    a further minute. Add the blanched nettles and the rest
    of the filling ingredients and cook until the mixture is
    starting to dry. Transfer to a large bowl and allow to
    cool slightly. Add the "cheese" and roughly combine
    with a spoon to a achieve a thick, crumbly filling.

04 Preheat the oven to 180°C/ 160°C fan /350°F/Gas 4.
    To assemble, grease a 23-cm/9-in square baking tin with a
    little of the oil. Keep the filo under a damp tea towel to
    retain moisture. Place one filo sheet in the prepared tin,
    allowing the excess to hang over the sides. Brush with oil.
    Repeat with three more layers of pastry, brushing with oil
    after each addition. Add the filling, spreading it in an even
    layer. Repeat the layered pastry technique with the
    remaining filo sheets, trimming the edges with scissors
    as needed. Coat the top layer with oil and sprinkle with
    nigella seeds. Bake for 45 minutes or until the top is flaky
    and golden brown. Cool for 10 minutes before serving.

Nettle and Pistachio Pesto Cornbread

Serves 4

Nettle pesto somehow tastes "greener" than basil pesto does – I don't know if it's because the nettles have a more earthy flavour or whether the act of foraging itself makes the end result feel closer to nature. The pistachios add another shade of green and a slightly sweet, perhaps somewhat exotic, aroma. You can use this pesto in the same way you would the more traditional stuff: with pasta, bruschetta, or sandwiches. I particularly like it baked into this cornbread, which has been one of my favourite loaves of bread ever since my stint living in the States. It has a gentle sweetness to it and a lovely crumbly texture. It works well as a side for a big (preferably green) stew, but also as a breakfast loaf with some vegan spread on top.

Ingredients

For the pesto
1½ tsp fine sea salt
150g/5½oz nettle leaves
2 garlic cloves, peeled and chopped
50g/1¾oz/heaped ⅓ cup pistachio
   kernels, chopped
3 tbsp nutritional yeast
juice and zest of ½ lemon
4 tbsp olive oil

For the cornbread
350ml/12fl oz/1½ cups full-fat
   or "barista" oat milk
2 tbsp apple cider vinegar
270g/9¾oz/1¾ cups polenta
110g/4oz/¾ cup + 2 tsp plain flour
2¼ tsp baking powder
1 heaped tsp bicarbonate of soda
1 heaped tsp fine sea salt
2 tbsp nutritional yeast
100ml/3½fl oz melted coconut oil,
   plus extra for greasing
150g/5½oz/¾ cup golden
   granulated sugar

Method

01   To prepare the nettles for the pesto, bring 2 litres/
3½ pints/8½ cups water with 1 teaspoon of the salt to
the boil in a large saucepan. Using gloves, carefully
add the nettles and blanch for 3 minutes. Remove using
a slotted spoon or tongs, or drain in a colander over
a bowl (save the blanching water for the nettle dye,
p82). Plunge the nettles into a bowl of cold water.
Once cool, drain and pat dry with a tea towel.

02   Combine the blanched nettles with the remaining pesto
ingredients in a pestle and mortar or a food processor.
I like getting the texture of my pesto to a thick-bodied
paste, but you may want to go smoother.

03   Next, prepare the bread. Pour the oat milk and vinegar
into a large bowl and whisk to combine. Leave to rest
for 10 minutes, allowing it to thicken and curdle to
buttermilk consistency.

04   Meanwhile, preheat the oven to 180°C/160°C
fan/350°F/Gas 4 and grease a 900-g/2-lb loaf tin with
a little melted coconut oil. In a separate large bowl, add
the polenta, flour, baking powder, bicarbonate of soda,
salt, and nutritional yeast. Stir to combine.

05   In a small bowl, whisk the coconut oil with the sugar
until thick and gooey. Add to the thickened oat milk
and whisk to combine. Add the dry ingredients to the
wet ingredients and whisk well to form a consistent,
smooth batter.

06   Pour the batter into the loaf tin. Using a spoon, dab
the pesto evenly over the poured batter. Now use
a butter knife to swirl the pesto into the batter.

07   Bake for 40–50 minutes until the centre has firmed up
and a skewer inserted into the centre comes out clean.
Leave to cool in the tin for 20 minutes, then turn out.
Cut into slices and serve.

Nettle Soup

Serves 6

Nettle pudding is one of the oldest recipes in the world (first recorded in Britain around 6,000BCE). While it inspired this dish, the ingredients aren't quite the same: the original relied on many other indigenous weeds and it certainly didn't include ground almonds! But there is something that feels quite primal in this soup – so nourishing, so heartwarming, and all from such a prevalent, readily available, and free ingredient. It's simple to make but has a surprising depth of flavour. I make it in the early stages of the nettle season, when it's cold and dark outside, to remind myself that spring is coming. It's a good substantial lunch or even a fuss-free winter dinner. If I don't have the time (or inclination) to make the crisps, I have it with a nice piece of sourdough toast.

Ingredients

For the soup
1½ tsp sea salt flakes
400g/14oz nettles (leaves and stalks, if tender enough)
2 tbsp olive oil
1 onion, peeled and chopped (save the skins for dyeing)
3 garlic cloves, peeled and finely chopped
1 leek, white part sliced (save the green top to make a vegetable stock)
3 carrots, peeled and chopped
2 potatoes, peeled and chopped
1.5 litres/2¾ pints/6 cups vegetable stock
100g/3½oz spinach

100g/3½oz/scant 1 cup ground almonds
2 tbsp nutritional yeast
juice of 1 lemon
oat cream, to serve (optional)
chopped parsley, to serve (optional)

For the tahini nettle crisps
2 tbsp raw tahini
1 tbsp olive oil
juice of ½ lemon
1 tsp nutritional yeast
1 tsp fine sea salt
40g/1½oz nettle leaves, washed

Blanching nettles

Blanching your nettles before adding them to recipes cleans them and removes their sting. It also helps to extract their colour for dyeing (pp82–85). Store the blanching water for your next dye vat in an airtight container in the freezer for up to 12 weeks.

Method

01 To prepare the nettles, bring 2 litres/3½ pints/8½ cups water with ½ tsp salt to the boil in a large saucepan. Using gloves, carefully add the nettles and blanch for 3 minutes. Remove using a slotted spoon or tongs (save the blanching water for the nettle dye, p82). Plunge the nettles into a bowl of cold water, then drain.

02 Heat the oil in a large saucepan over medium heat. Lower the heat, add the onions and cook for 5–7 minutes, until translucent. Add the garlic and cook for another minute. Add the leek, carrot, and potatoes and cook for 10 minutes, stirring occasionally. Add the stock, bring to boil, then simmer for 10–15 mins until the potatoes have softened.

03 Meanwhile, make the crisps. Preheat the oven to 180°C/ 160°C fan/350°F/Gas 4 and line a large baking tray with greaseproof paper. In a large bowl, combine the tahini, oil, lemon juice, nutritional yeast, and salt. Wearing gloves, place the nettles in the bowl and toss and rub the tahini dressing into the leaves until coated evenly. Transfer to the lined tray and spread the leaves across in a single layer. Bake for 10 minutes, then flip the leaves and return to the oven for another 10 minutes until crisp. Remove from the oven and leave to cool.

04 Add the blanched nettles and spinach to the soup and simmer for another 5 minutes. Remove from heat and purée the soup using a hand-held blender. Return the soup to a low heat and stir in the ground almonds, nutritional yeast, remaining salt and lemon juice. Serve topped with a handful of the nettle crisps or a splash of oat cream and some chopped parsley.

Nettle-and-Herb-Stuffed Bread

Serves 4

This loaf is the unlikely love child of Italian focaccia bread and the savoury Turkish pastry börek. Baking it is a matter of delicate balance, getting the top just brown enough (but not burnt!) so that it has a slightly crispy crust while keeping the inside soft and airy. Watch it closely as you get to the end of the baking time and don't be scared to push the crust a bit too close to the edge. You can, by all means, only use white bread flour in this recipe, but I find that the wholemeal elicits a slightly nutty flavour from the nettles and helps to achieve a more engaging, slightly gooey texture, which gives a little boost to its desirable tanned appearance.

Ingredients

For the dough
200g/7oz/1½ cups strong wholemeal bread flour
250g/9oz/2 cups strong white bread flour, plus extra for dusting
1 tbsp dried active yeast
1 tbsp nutritional yeast
1½ tsp fine sea salt
4 tbsp olive oil, plus extra for greasing
3 tbsp date molasses

For the filling
2 tsp sea salt flakes
175g/6oz nettle leaves and tender stems
2 tbsp olive oil

1 onion, peeled and chopped (save the skins for dyeing)
2 garlic cloves, peeled and finely chopped, or 20g/¾oz wild garlic, peeled and finely chopped, if available
20g/¾oz parsley leaves, chopped
20g/¾oz mint leaves, chopped
20g/¾oz dill, chopped
juice of ½ lemon

To assemble
2 tbsp olive oil
2 tsp nigella seeds
1 tsp sea salt flakes

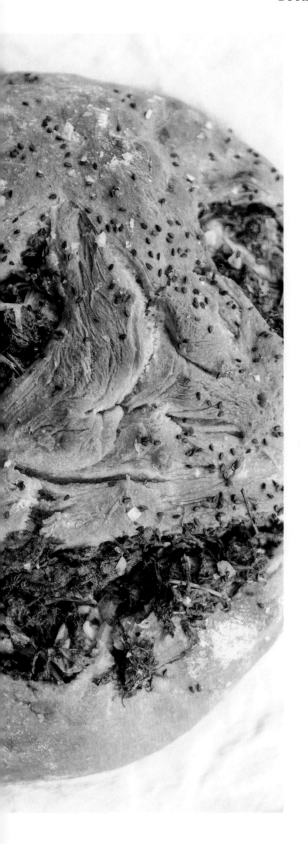

Method

01 Make the dough. In a large mixing bowl, combine the flours, yeast, nutritional yeast, and salt. Add the oil and molasses. Start to combine, using your hands or the bread attachment of a food processor, while gradually adding 200ml/7fl oz/scant 1 cup lukewarm water. Once the dough comes together, tip it out onto a floured work surface and knead by hand for 5 minutes, or mix on medium speed for 5 minutes in a food processor. Place it in a well-greased bowl and cover with a damp tea towel. Leave to rise for 1–2 hours or until doubled in size.

02 While the dough is rising, prepare the filling. Bring 2 litres/3½ pints/8½ cups water with 1 teaspoon of the salt to the boil in a large saucepan. Using gloves, carefully add the nettles and blanch for 3 minutes. Remove using a slotted spoon or tongs, or drain in a colander over a bowl (save the blanching water for the nettle dye, p82). Plunge the nettles into a bowl of cold water. Once cool, drain and pat dry with a tea towel.

03 Heat the oil in a large frying pan over a medium-high heat. Lower the heat, add the onion and cook for 3 minutes. If using garlic, add and cook for a further minute. If you are lucky enough to get a hold of some wild garlic, add it alongside the blanched nettles and the rest of the filling ingredients. Cook for 3 minutes, stirring or tossing frequently. Remove from the heat and allow to cool.

04 Heat the oven to 220°C/200°C fan/425°F/Gas 7 and line a large baking tray with greaseproof paper. Tip the dough onto a floured work surface and roll into a 50 x 20-cm/20 x 8-in rectangle, about 1cm/½in thick.

05 To assemble the loaf, spread the filling evenly down the centre of the rectangle (from short edge to short edge) and sprinkle with half of the oil, nigella seeds, and salt. Pinch the long edges of the dough together, covering the filling, at 10cm/4in intervals along the length of the rectangle. Slowly, roll the dough into a pinwheel – it's a bit fiddly, so don't worry about getting the shape completely even. No matter how out of balance it may look, it always forms a glorious ammonite shape once baked.

06 Carefully transfer the loaf to the lined tray and sprinkle the remaining oil, nigella seeds and salt over the top. Bake for 30–40 minutes, or until the top and bottom of the loaf is golden and just starting to brown. Cool on a wire rack and serve warm or at room temperature.

Dye with *Nettle*

All dye plants produce different shades throughout the season, which makes complete sense when you think about it. After all, this is the way colours evolve – and die out – in nature. Nettle is the plant that showcases this better than most when you dye with it. Rather than mordants and different dye "cocktail mixers", it is ultimately the time in the season that will determine your shade.

The best thing about dyeing with nettle is the abundance of it. Even after cooking with it – using your own or one of the recipes in this book (pp72–81), there will be enough foliage left to strengthen the blanching water for your dye vat using just the bottom, less edible, leaves of the plants you have foraged, or even leaves from plants that have gone to seed. This is the reason I chose it for the duster, a long light coat (really a spring-summer jacket) that requires quite a lot of dyestuff.

If you are willing to embrace the serendipity of dyeing it after you've sewn it, accepting that the dye may strike unevenly, you will need a rather large pot. Alternatively, for more control over the final result, you can pre-dye your fabric (just make sure that the lengths are big enough to cut all the different pattern pieces from).

Dye methods

To get a more vibrant shade of the colours (pp84–85), simply add more leaves (and stalks) to the water in your dye vat. Once you have added everything, bring to the boil and then remove from the heat source and let the nettle steep for 24 hours. Strain to remove the dyestuff, then add your fabric to the dye vat and bring to the boil. Remove the vat from the heat and leave the fabric to absorb the dye overnight or for up to 24 hours.

Nettle is also suitable for an "all-in-one" dye method in which the dyestuff and the fabric are added to the vat at the same time. First steep the leaves for an hour, then add the cloth. As the dyestuff cools and disintegrates it will create random patterns across the fabric surface, as the areas that come into direct contact with the plant material will absorb more colour and may even become dotted with sub-shades of the dominant pigments.

....

Upcycling ramie fabric

Most of the Nettle Dusters featured on the following pages are made of antique French linen. However, I couldn't resist the urge to work with ramie. Originating from the nettle family and most commonly grown in Asia, ramie is one of the most ancient fibre crops, used for over 6,000 years. Often mistaken for linen, ramie is softer but stronger. It also takes less dye to achieve the same depth of colour than you would need when working with genuine linen. Ramie can be deemed a "sustainable" fabric (as long as it's not blended with other, unsustainable fibres) as, unlike cotton, there is no need to use chemical fertilizers or large amounts of water to grow it. However, the processing of the fibre requires a lot of energy and the use of chemicals. Like many other fibres originating in the Far East, the workers who harvest these plants often suffer from poor and sometimes unsafe working conditions. It took a bit of research, but I managed to find some ramie to upcycle: an old Ikea bed sheet bought online. I used it to make a shorter version of the duster (p88).

....

Rich tones

Nettle is rich in chlorophyll, the natural green pigment found in leafy plants. For this reason, it has been historically used to achieve an array of green shades. The earlier you pick the plant, the greener your fabric will become. The quality of the colour varies depending on the health of the plant and the richness of the soil it grows in. Even periods of frost, expected at the beginning of the nettle season, can alter the colour of the leaves, giving them a faint purplish tint. If I want to get close to emerald green, I add chlorophyll extract (a common dietary supplement) to the dye vat, alongside an alum mordant.

In the later stages of the season, when the nettle leaves obtain a more yellowish hue, I incorporate some chlorophyll to my dyes to reach olive shades. For a more naive quality of green, I extract blue pigment from woad leaves, an easy-care indigeonous plant that I always grow amongst my flowers. Adding woad-infused water (p22) to the dye vat creates a lighter shade – think 1970s denim, but green. Sometimes, when I add woad to my late-spring or summer foraged nettles, I also introduce coffee grounds to the vat, or replace the alum mordant with an iron one to make the colours muddier.

Warm and cool tones

Greyish-green with a sweet, cool quality – the colour equivalent of the taste of mint – can be obtained in the spring by steeping (mordanted) fabric in a good amount of nettle blanching water after it has cooled down. (If you are dyeing several pieces of cloth, replace the water with fresh blanching water each time to prevent the shade becoming too faint.) The same method will work in the summer to achieve a light khaki or dirty pale yellow. Stems picked in late summer will give you a more substantial khaki or warm tans – these will particularly benefit from the addition of iron mordant to the dye vat, which enriches these sombre tones. If you are adding just a small amount of nettles to modify the colour, make sure to pre-mordant the fabric beforehand with alum or bind with plant-based milk.

Much as their name suggests, dyeing with dead-nettles will result in a more subdued array of colours. Following the same preparation methods, the colour you will get is what I can only describe as a dead shade of beige yellow. Adding iron will modify this to a grey-olive, which will become more pronounced if you add some leaves of the two other nettle types to the mix.

See pages 18–23 for more detailed information on techniques, dyestuff, mordants, and dye vat ratios.

During the First World War, nettles were used to dye German military uniforms and were a source of many camouflage hues. Their leaves and stalks produce a spectrum of colours that blend seamlessly into their natural habitats – fields, woodlands, and moors.

Nettle colour range

The short, ramie version of the Nettle Duster (p88) weighs around 250g (9oz), while the full-length jacket may, in medium-heavy antique linen, reach 750g (1lb 10oz). These tentative dye "recipes" are for 100g (3½oz) of fabric – multiply the quantities as required and use enough water to cover the fabric. Bear in mind that the shade may vary depending on your fabric, water pH level, time in the foraging season, soil health, and serendipity.

Emerald-ish green

Medium-weight antique linen, bound with almond milk and mordanted with alum. Dyed with nettle blanching water, strengthened with 150g (5½oz) of first spring nettle tops and ½ tsp of chlorophyllin powder for every 100g (3½oz) of fabric. Boiled and simmered for 3 hours, left to steep overnight.

Sea green

Medium-weight coarse antique linen, mordanted with alum. Dyed with nettle blanching water, strengthened with 100g (3½oz) of mid-spring nettle leaves and stalks and a scant pinch of chlorophyllin for every 100g (3½oz) of fabric. Boiled and simmered for 2 hours, left to steep overnight.

Sage green

Lightweight ramie, bound with almond milk and mordanted with alum. Dyed with nettle blanching water, strengthened with 100g (3½oz) of late spring nettle leaves and stalks and 4 tbsp of woad-infused water for every 100g (3½oz) of fabric. Boiled and simmered for 3 hours, left to steep for 12 hours.

Dye Nettle

Darkish grey

Lightweight linen mordanted with alum. Dyed in an aluminium vat with nettle blanching water, strengthened with 120g (4oz) of late spring nettle leaves and stalks and 2 tbsp of iron water for every 100g (3½oz) of fabric. Boiled and simmered for 2 hours, left to steep for 8 hours.

Greyish mint

Lightweight ramie, bound with oat milk and mordanted with alum. Dyed with the blanching water from nettle leaves (120g (4oz) of nettles for every 100g (3½oz)of fabric), left to steep for 48 hours.

Khaki

Medium-weight organic cotton drill bound with oat milk. Dyed with nettle blanching water, strengthened with 120g (4oz) of early summer nettle leaves and stalks and 1 tbsp of iron sulphate powder for every 100g (3½oz) of fabric. Boiled and simmered for 2 hours, left to steep for 6 hours.

Dirty beige

Medium-weight French linen. Dyed with 100g (3½oz) of dead nettles for every 100g (3½oz) of fabric. Boiled and simmered for 3 hours, left to steep for 48 hours.

The Nettle Duster

The Nettle Duster is the first of several gender-neutral pieces featured in this book. Previously referred to as "his&hers" or unisex garments, an extensive discussion surrounds these clothes in their current incarnation. Fashion is always at its best when it involves significant cultural debates and plays a role in altering our perception. It's part of why I chose to feature these non-binary cuts, but to be honest I like designing (and wearing) them because they are just so effortlessly cool. While they are the opposite of figure-hugging, which is part of their charm, I would still encourage you to consider some light adaptations to tailor them to your frame.

Construction

Shown on the right are the pattern pieces for the Nettle Duster (please see Pattern Sheets 5 and 6).

You'll also require 6-7 buttons, at least 2.5cm (1in) in diameter – 4-5 for the centre front and 2 for the back belt – as well as 6m (6½ yards) of 18mm (¹¹⁄₁₆in) bias binding. Buy it folded, or follow the instructions on p58, step 07.

All seam allowances are 1cm (⅜in) unless otherwise stated

Measurements

This is a relaxed-fitting long jacket, with an oversized front piece, pushing the side seam towards the back.

Please refer to the appendix on p219 for size charts and fabric requirements. To determine the right size for you, cross reference your bust/chest, waist, and hip measurements.

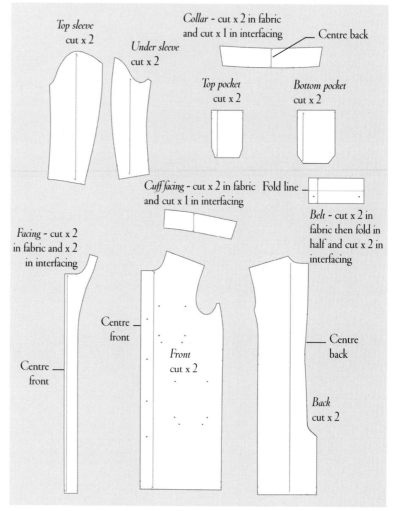

Pattern pieces

Method

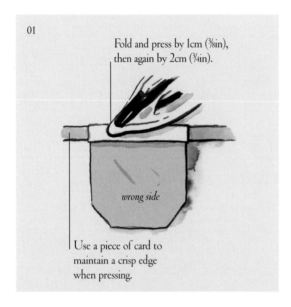

01

Fold and press by 1cm (⅜in), then again by 2cm (¾in).

wrong side

Use a piece of card to maintain a crisp edge when pressing.

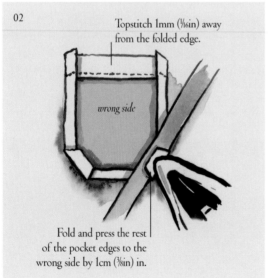

02

Topstitch 1mm (¹⁄₁₆in) away from the folded edge.

wrong side

Fold and press the rest of the pocket edges to the wrong side by 1cm (⅜in) in.

01 **Prepare the pockets**

This duster coat features two top pockets: one external, on the left-hand side of the chest, and one (optional) internal pocket, on the right-hand side. It also features two larger bottom pockets on the hip area. These instructions apply to all the pockets.

Fold and press the top edge of the pocket to the wrong side by 1cm (⅜in). Fold and press this edge over again by 2cm (¾in).

02 Topstitch 1mm (¹⁄₁₆in) away from the folded edge, positioning the inside edge of your machine foot on the fold line as a guide.

Fold and press the rest of the pocket edges to the wrong side by 1cm (⅜in) in, working your way down from the side edges.

Nettle Jacket

You could make this coat into a shorter jacket by bringing the hemline up by roughly 40cm (16in) and sewing the lower pockets about 8cm (3in) above the hem. If you are quite petite, you might also want to consider replacing the back belt with back ties by adding at least 50cm (20in) to the belt pattern piece. This will allow you to cinch the waist further and makes for a more feminine style.

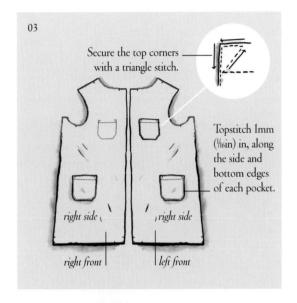

03

Secure the top corners with a triangle stitch.

Topstitch 1mm (¹⁄₁₆in) in, along the side and bottom edges of each pocket.

right side   *right side*

right front   *left front*

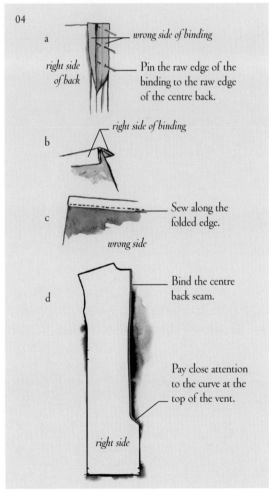

04

a

right side of back

wrong side of binding

Pin the raw edge of the binding to the raw edge of the centre back.

b

right side of binding

c

Sew along the folded edge.

wrong side

d

Bind the centre back seam.

Pay close attention to the curve at the top of the vent.

right side

03 Attach the pockets to the front pieces

Pin the pockets in place on the front pieces according to the markings on the pattern. (If you are opting for the shorter jacket version, place the lower pockets 8cm (3in) above the hem line). Using the pocket edge as a guide, topstitch 1mm (¹⁄₁₆in) in, along the side and bottom edges of each pocket. For longevity, secure the top corners with a triangle stitch: sew a couple of stitches, sink your needle into the fabric, and pivot. Sew a few more stitches, pivot again, and sew the remaining side of the triangle. Pivot once more, sewing over the first set of stitches to fully secure the triangle in place. Press. Repeat for the internal pocket, if required.

04 Bind the centre back seam

Open out the bias binding. With right sides together, aligning the raw edges, pin the bias binding to the centre back. Sew together, stitching along the pressed line.

Fold the binding over the raw edge of the back piece to the wrong side (b). Sew along the folded edge of the binding to secure in place (c) – see p59 for more details. Pay close attention as you curve the binding around the pivot point at the top of the vent (d). Repeat for the other back piece.

NOTE: It's incredibly easy to stretch bias binding even as you apply it to straight lines cut on the fabric's straight grain. Stitching binding to lines cut on the inherently stretchy bias, which runs diagonally to the grain, can be doubly challenging. Sew it carefully. For a simpler finish, use an overlock or zigzag stitch to finish the centre back seam.

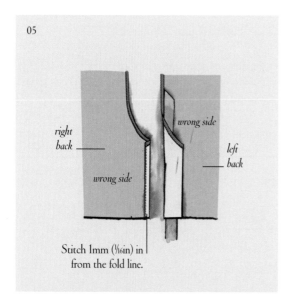

05

right back

wrong side

wrong side

left back

Stitch 1mm (¹⁄₁₆in) in from the fold line.

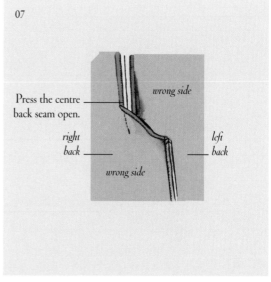

07

Press the centre back seam open.

wrong side

right back

left back

wrong side

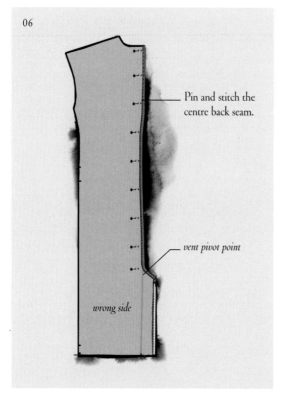

06

Pin and stitch the centre back seam.

vent pivot point

wrong side

05 **Sew the vent**

On the bottom of both back pieces, fold and press the vent line to the wrong side of the fabric by 7mm (¼in). Fold and press by another 7mm (¼in).

Then, on the right back piece only: stitch 1mm (¹⁄₁₆in) in from the fold line, using the inside edge of your machine foot as a guide.

On the left back piece only: fold the vent to the wrong side by 4cm (1⅝in), so that the fold is in line with the bound edge above, and press. You may choose to use the card method to achieve a crisp fold line.

06 Pin the two back pieces right sides together and stitch the centre back seam, finishing at the vent pivot point, as marked on the pattern.

07 Press the centre back seam open.

08

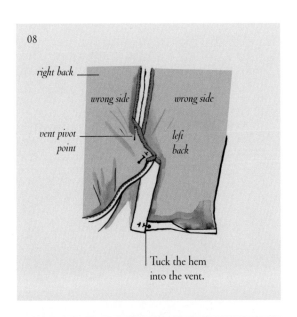

right back

wrong side   wrong side

vent pivot
point   left
                     back

Tuck the hem
into the vent.

10

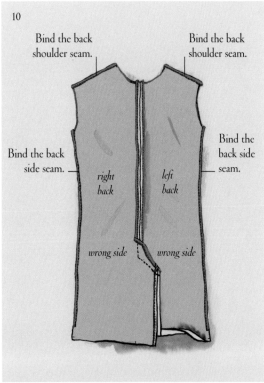

Bind the back
shoulder seam.

Bind the back
shoulder seam.

Bind the back
side seam.

right
back

left
back

Bind the
back side
seam.

wrong side   wrong side

09

a

Stitch the top of
the vent 1cm (⅜in)
in from the
bound edge.

wrong side

right
back   wrong side

left
back

b

vent line

08 On the left back piece only: Fold and press the hem to the wrong side, first by 1cm (⅜in) and then by another 2.5cm (¾in). Tuck the hem into the vent.

09 On the right back piece, with the wrong side of the fabric facing up, stitch the top of the vent 1cm (⅜in) in from the bound edge (a). As you reach the pivot point (marked in red on the illustration), leave the machine needle in the fabric and move the right back piece out of the way so that the left piece, featuring the 4cm (1⅝in) vent fold, is facing up (b). Pivot and stitch the vent line 1mm (⅟₁₆in) in from the folded edge, using the inside edge of your machine foot as a guide. The inset illustration (b) shows the outcome on the right side of the fabric.

10 **Bind the back sides and shoulder seams**
Bind the back side and shoulder seams following the instructions in step 4 or finish with an overlock or zigzag stitch. To avoid bulk in the hem fold, do not bind the hemline.

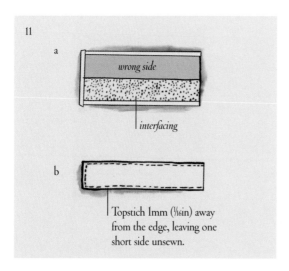

a

wrong side

interfacing

b

Topstitch 1mm (¹⁄₁₆in) away
from the edge, leaving one
short side unsewn.

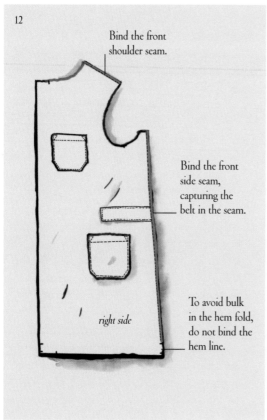

Bind the front
shoulder seam.

Bind the front
side seam,
capturing the
belt in the seam.

right side

To avoid bulk
in the hem fold,
do not bind the
hem line.

11 Sew the belt

Apply interfacing to the bottom wrong side of the belt
pieces. Press the top, bottom, and side seam allowances
to the wrong side (a). Fold the belt in half, wrong sides
together. Topstitch 1mm (¹⁄₁₆in) away from the edge,
leaving one short side unsewn (b).

12 Bind the front side and shoulder seams

As the belt is sewn into the side seam, pin the belt
pieces to the right side of the front according to the
notches marked on the pattern, aligning the unstitched
short end of the belt with the raw edge of the front.
Stitch across the belt, 7mm (¹⁄₄in) away from the edge.
Bind the front side seams following the instructions
in step 4. To avoid bulk in the hem fold, do not bind
the hemline.

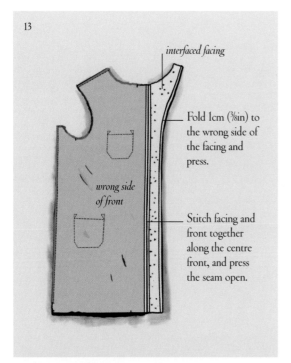

13

interfaced facing

*wrong side
of front*

Fold 1cm (⅜in) to
the wrong side of
the facing and
press.

Stitch facing and
front together
along the centre
front, and press
the seam open.

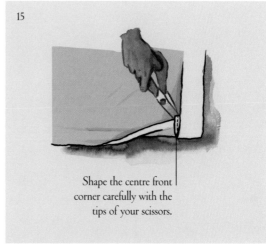

15

Shape the centre front
corner carefully with the
tips of your scissors.

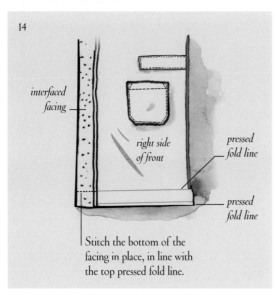

14

*interfaced
facing*

*right side
of front*

*pressed
fold line*

*pressed
fold line*

Stitch the bottom of the
facing in place, in line with
the top pressed fold line.

13 Sew the facing

Apply interfacing to the wrong side of the facing.
Topstitch 1cm (⅜in) away from the edge of the curved
part of the facing piece. Fold the facing to the wrong side
of the fabric along the stitching line and press. Pin together
the centre front lines of the facing and front body piece so
the right sides are facing together. Stitch 1cm (⅜in) away
from the edge. Press the seam allowance open.

14 Fold and press the hem: first by 1cm (⅜in) towards the
wrong side of the fabric, then fold and press by another
2.5cm (¾in). Fold the facing towards the front body piece
so the right sides are together. Stitch the bottom of the
facing in place 3.5cm (1⅜in) above the bottom edge,
following the top fold line.

15 Fold the facing to the wrong side of the front, hiding the
interfacing. Push the seam allowance of the hem behind
the facing. Trim as necessary if the seam is getting too
bulky. Shape the centre front corner carefully with the
tips of your scissors. Press the entire facing area, paying
particular attention to the centre front seam. Repeat steps
13–15 for the other front and facing pieces. (We will return
to the facing once the collar has been sewn in step 21.)

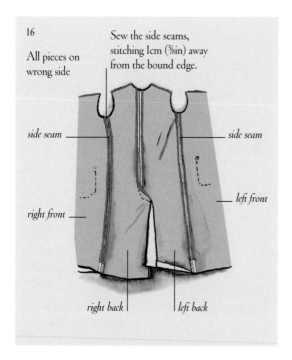

16

All pieces on wrong side

Sew the side seams, stitching 1cm (⅜in) away from the bound edge.

side seam

side seam

left front

right front

right back | left back

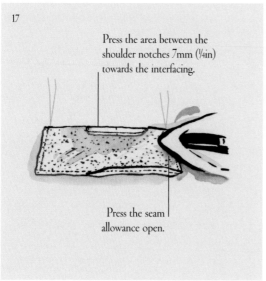

17

Press the area between the shoulder notches 7mm (¼in) towards the interfacing.

Press the seam allowance open.

16 **Sew the side seams**

Pin the front and back right sides together along the side seams and sew, keeping the folded hem open as you stitch. Press the seams open. Press well from both sides and press the hem fold back in place.

17 **Sew the collar**

Apply interfacing to the wrong side of one collar piece; this will be the top collar. Press the area between the shoulder notches towards the interfacing by 7mm (¼in). Pin the top collar to the under collar right sides together and the wrong sides are facing out. Stitch around three sides 7mm (¼in) from the edge, leaving the side with the 7mm (¼in) pressed area unstitched.

When you are one stitch away from the pivot points (marked in red on the illustration), keep your machine needle in the fabric, lift the presser foot, and insert a length of doubled thread, wrapping it tightly against the needle. Lower the foot, then slowly make a single stitch over the thread. Leave the needle down and pull the thread on the right side over to the left, around the base of the needle, so that both lengths are pulled towards the bottom of the collar. Leave the needle down and turn the collar, ready to sew the next side. Pivot and sew a single stitch to "trap" the thread tail in between the two stitches that make the corner. This hack will help you achieve a sharp corner – see p137 for more details.

Once stitched, press the seam allowance open.

18

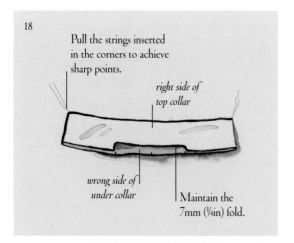

Pull the strings inserted
in the corners to achieve
sharp points.

*right side of
top collar*

*wrong side of
under collar*

Maintain the
7mm (¼in) fold.

20

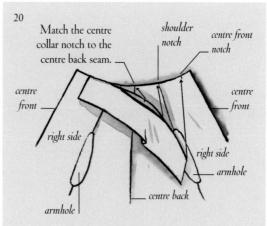

Match the centre
collar notch to the
centre back seam.

*shoulder
notch*

*centre front
notch*

*centre
front*

*centre
front*

right side

right side

armhole

centre back

armhole

19

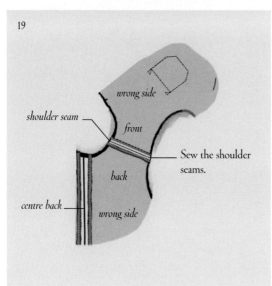

wrong side

shoulder seam

front

back

Sew the shoulder
seams.

centre back

wrong side

18 Turn the collar right side out and pull the threads
    inserted in the corners to achieve sharp points.
    Press well, maintaining the 7mm (¼in) fold at the
    bottom edge.

19 Sew the shoulder seams

    Pin the front and back together at the shoulder seams,
    right sides together, and stitch. Press the seams open.

20 Attach the collar to the body

    Place the under collar (the non-interfaced layer) against
    the right side of the front and pin the three layers
    (front, under collar, top collar) in place from the centre
    front notches to the shoulders. Between the shoulders,
    pin the under collar layer only to the back of the
    neckline, leaving the top collar with the pressed seam
    allowance loose. Stitch 7mm (¼in) away from the collar
    edge, carefully separating the top collar from the stitch
    line along the folded area.

    Cut a notch in at the shoulder points and push the
    seam allowance inside the collar piece. Press.

21

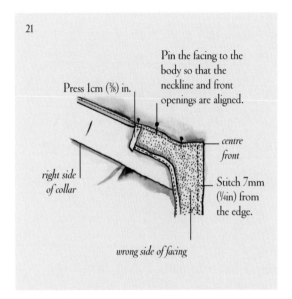

Press 1cm (⅜) in.

Pin the facing to the body so that the neckline and front openings are aligned.

right side of collar

centre front

Stitch 7mm (¼in) from the edge.

wrong side of facing

23

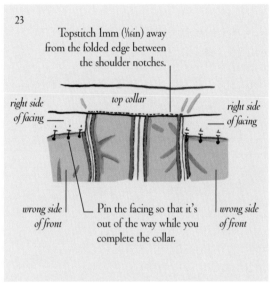

Topstitch 1mm (¹⁄₁₆in) away from the folded edge between the shoulder notches.

right side of facing

top collar

right side of facing

wrong side of front

Pin the facing so that it's out of the way while you complete the collar.

wrong side of front

22

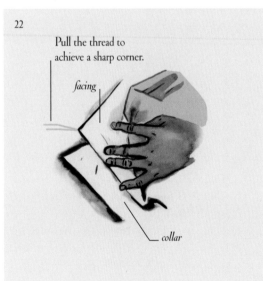

Pull the thread to achieve a sharp corner.

facing

collar

21 **Attach the facing to the neckline**
Press the facing shoulder line to the wrong side of the fabric by 1cm (⅜in). With right sides together, aligning the neckline and front opening, pin the facing to the front. The collar is sandwiched between the body and the facing. Stitch 7mm (¼in) from the edge. Repeat the threaded corner technique from step 17 for the centre front corner. Cut notches into the curved seam and trim the corner.

22 Bag out and pull the thread for a sharp point. Press well. Repeat steps 21–22 for the other side.

23 **Complete the collar**
Pin the facing out of the way while you complete the collar. Topstitch the top collar down, 1mm (¹⁄₁₆in) away from the folded edge, so that the back neckline is sandwiched between the collar pieces. Press well.

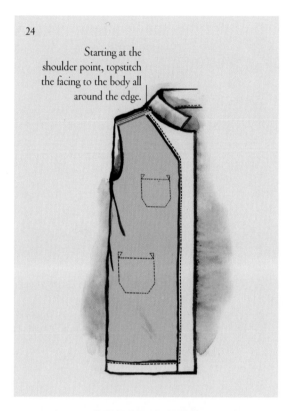

24

Starting at the shoulder point, topstitch the facing to the body all around the edge.

24 Complete the facing

Pin the curved line of the facing to the body of the coat, all the way down to the hem. Starting at the shoulder point, topstitch the pinned facing line to the body all around 1mm (¹⁄₁₆in) from the edge, pivoting as you reach the bottom to stitch the hem, and then pivoting again to stitch the remaining facing piece, until you reach the opposite shoulder from the one you started from.

NOTE: the shoulder edge of the facing (shown in yellow on the illustration) remains unstitched, as it is held in place by the collar and the facing stitch.

25 Press well. Pay special attention to the neckline, holding the collar up and pressing as close as you can to the seam.

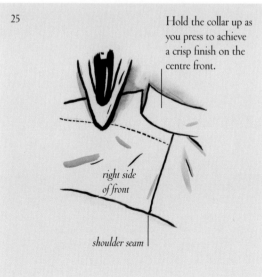

25

Hold the collar up as you press to achieve a crisp finish on the centre front.

right side of front

shoulder seam

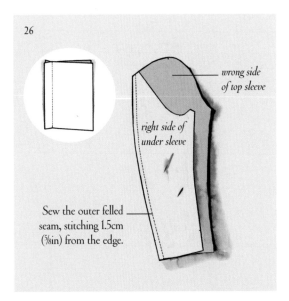

26

wrong side of top sleeve

right side of under sleeve

Sew the outer felled seam, stitching 1.5cm (⅝in) from the edge.

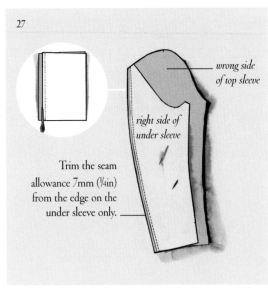

27

wrong side of top sleeve

right side of under sleeve

Trim the seam allowance 7mm (¼in) from the edge on the under sleeve only.

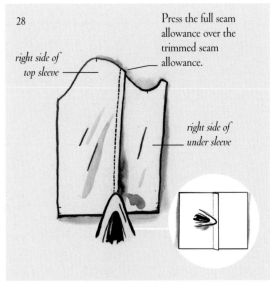

28

Press the full seam allowance over the trimmed seam allowance.

right side of top sleeve

right side of under sleeve

26 **Sew the sleeves**
Start with the outer felled seam. Pin the top sleeve and under sleeve along the longer seam, wrong sides together and stitch, taking a 1.5-cm (⅝-in) seam allowance.

27 On the under sleeve, trim the seam allowance down to 7mm (¼in).

28 Press the seam allowance towards the under sleeve.

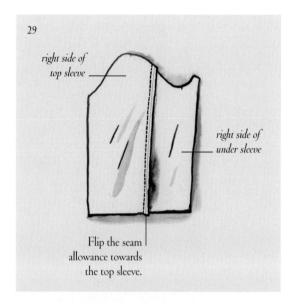

29

right side of top sleeve

right side of under sleeve

Flip the seam allowance towards the top sleeve.

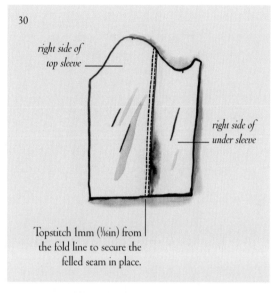

30

right side of top sleeve

right side of under sleeve

Topstitch 1mm (⅟₁₆in) from the fold line to secure the felled seam in place.

FELLED SEAM TECHNIQUE CONTINUED

a

wrong side

Flip the seam allowance towards the top sleeve.

right side   *right side*

b

right side   *right side*

Fold and press the wider section of the seam allowance in half and cover the trimmed section.

c

right side   *right side*

Flip the seam allowance back towards the under sleeve so all the raw edges are concealed.

1mm (⅟₁₆in) from fold line.

29 Flip the seam allowance towards the top sleeve and fold and press the wider section of the seam allowance in half, so that it covers the trimmed section. Take your time to get this even and consistent.

30 Flip the seam allowance back towards the under sleeve, so that all the raw edges are concealed. Topstitch 1mm (⅟₁₆in) in from the fold line to secure the felled seam in place. Press well. Repeat steps 26–30 for the other sleeve.

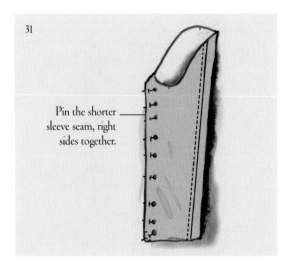

31

Pin the shorter sleeve seam, right sides together.

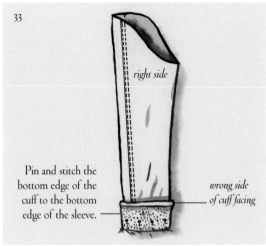

33

right side

Pin and stitch the bottom edge of the cuff to the bottom edge of the sleeve.

wrong side of cuff facing

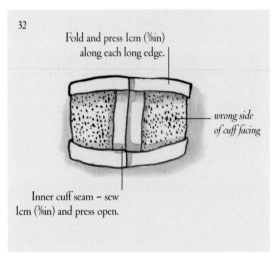

32

Fold and press 1cm (⅜in) along each long edge.

wrong side of cuff facing

Inner cuff seam – sew 1cm (⅜in) and press open.

31 Sew the inner sleeve seam

Pin the shorter sleeve seam, right sides together, and stitch. Finish the seam with an overlock or zigzag stitch.

32 Sew the cuffs

Apply interfacing to the wrong side of the cuff facing. Along each long edge, fold and press 1cm (⅜in) to the wrong side. Unfold the folds, then pin and stitch the short cuff facing edges right sides together. Press the seam open. Repeat for the other cuff facing.

33 Attach the cuff to the sleeve

With right sides together, matching the cuff facing seam to the shorter (inner) sleeve seam, pin and stitch the bottom edge of the cuff to the bottom edge of the sleeve, stitching along the fold line pressed in step 32. Press the seam open. Repeat for the other sleeve and cuff facing.

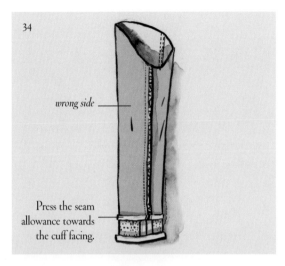

34

wrong side —

Press the seam
allowance towards
the cuff facing.

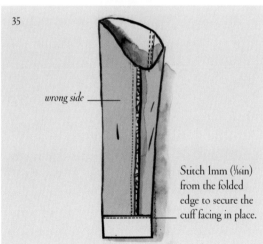

35

wrong side —

Stitch 1mm (¹⁄₁₆in)
from the folded
edge to secure the
cuff facing in place.

34 Turn the sleeve inside out and pull out the cuff facing
so that the wrong side of both the sleeve and the facing
are facing out. Press the seam towards the facing.

35 Fold the cuff facing to the wrong side of the sleeve, so
that the wrong sides are together. Keep the top edge of
the facing folded in and pin in place. Stitch 1mm (¹⁄₁₆in)
from the edge to secure the cuff facing in place. Press.
Repeat for the other sleeve.

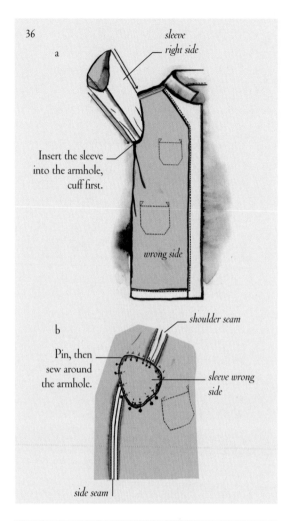

36

a

sleeve
right side

Insert the sleeve
into the armhole,
cuff first.

wrong side

b

shoulder seam

Pin, then
sew around
the armhole.

sleeve wrong
side

side seam

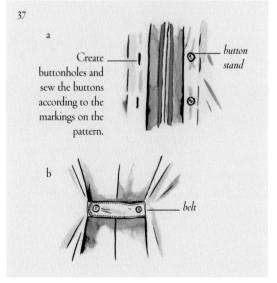

37

a

Create
buttonholes and
sew the buttons
according to the
markings on the
pattern.

button
stand

b

belt

36 Attach the sleeves to the body

With right sides together, insert the sleeve into the arm hole, cuff first (a), matching the sleeve seams and sleeve head notches at the top of the sleeve. Pin together, then sew in in place (b). As this is a relaxed drop shoulder fit, there is no need to ease the sleeve head. Finish with an overlock or zigzag stitch and press well, using a sleeve board if you have one (or a rolled towel). Repeat for the other sleeve.

37 Sew the buttonholes and buttons

Following your machine instructions and the markings on the pattern, make buttonholes and sew buttons on both the button stand at the front (a) and the belt at the back (b). Alternatively, sew on snap buttons.

....

Shoulder measurement and arm length

The arm length of the duster usually needs to be larger for men and shorter for women. This style was cut to accommodate both, so it's always on the longer side, but to make sure that it fits unique frame, pin the sleeve to the body after step 30, before you start sewing the cuff. Try the coat on, and remove excess fabric as necessary.

....

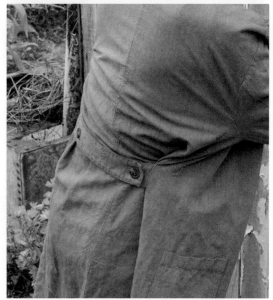

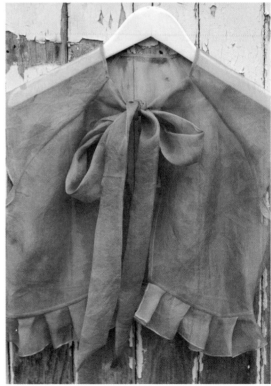

Rhubarb

I didn't grow up with rhubarb. In fact, I didn't even know it existed before I turned 18. My inaugural rhubarb was part of a mixed fruit crumble at the beloved Food for Thought – a legendary vegetarian restaurant in London, which sadly closed its doors in 2015 after decades of service. It was like nothing I'd experienced before: bold and tart and celery-like in texture and appearance, except in the most heart-rending shade of pink. I have been fascinated with rhubarb ever since. My enchantment only grew when I started dyeing, for rhubarb is one of the most hardworking plants in the natural dyer's arsenal. It was a revelation: the poisonous leaves, previously discarded before cooking due to the high concentration of oxalic acid, became a valuable source of natural mordant. The crown, which forms the plant base, was unveiled as a cache of stunning earthy tones. It is a true zero-waste plant. What's more, it is an incredibly easy crop to grow, one that will thrive in (substantial) containers and can even take a lot of shade. As a hardy perennial, once the plant has been established, it will keep on producing for years, reliably revealing its dazzling buds in the dark of winter, reminding us that spring is nigh.

Plant and cultivate *Rhubarb*

*Everything that I know about rhubarb I learnt from my friend Ged.
If you can call me a rhubarb enthusiast, then Ged is the rhubarb
wizard. It isn't just the sheer volume that he grows (three of the beds at
his picturesque plot in rural East Anglia are filled with copious amounts
of the stuff), it is the attention he dedicates to these plants, which is
rooted in his genuine admiration for and, I believe, affinity with them.
Ged speaks to his rhubarb. He tells tales, informs it about the weather
or what he has been up to on that day – like you would a friend...*

When we visited Ged and his amazing crop, my
photographer Julius pointed out that it's probably not only
Ged's words of encouragement that make his rhubarb thrive.
"If you care enough about your plants that you find the time
to talk to them, you're unlikely to just stop at that." Julius
was right. Ged always keeps his rhubarb in optimal
conditions. When we met him, on a warm July morning
towards the end of the growing season, his rhubarb looked
perky and protruding as ever. He told us how he fed it
throughout spring with his organic seaweed fertilizer, kept
weeds away, retained moisture by mulching around the
crowns (the parts of the plants that are visible at ground level
and reside just below), and watered it religiously. Rhubarb
requires a lot of it to grow, particularly if you grow water in
full sun as Ged does. He demonstrated how he keeps it
moist, holding his watering can high up, nearly 1.8m (6ft)
above the soil, and capping the spout with a rose attachment.

I have four rhubarb plants on my plot– a much more
modest yield than Ged's, but still enough to sustain me,
my dye habit, and all of my rhubarb-loving neighbours.
The healthiest is, naturally, the one that emerged from a
crown I got from Ged. This is one of the wonderful
things about rhubarb; it's a plant that encourages sharing.
Once it establishes, this hardy perennial will keep on
growing for years, sometimes even decades.

Ged allows the droplets to fall like raindrops while the arrow-shaped curly leaves, purposely designed by nature, keep the water dripping at just the right rate.

Still, every five years, as the plant gets congested, you need to lift it from the ground and split the crown. This results in embryonic plants, which, in my experience, are the best way to start growing rhubarb. You can also purchase crowns, or grow from seed – a much lengthier and laborious process. If you know anyone who grows rhubarb (or even inherited a plant, as they will often keep on growing in gardens without much special care), pay them a visit in late autumn, once the plant goes dormant.

Lift the crown up with a spade and, using a hoe, split it into three or four pieces, ensuring each one has thick roots as well as a large bud – an eye-shaped bulge – which will become your first shoot in the new year. Keep the budless, most tired parts of the original crown, pieces that would often get discarded, for your dye vat. Dividing the plant will also give you firsthand experience of this critical maintenance stage and you'll need to repeat this process once your plant reaches similar maturity.

When I planted the crown Ged gave to me, I listened to his advice. I chose a patch of rich, beefy soil, an area I stored manure in during my first winter on the site. I made sure there were no deep-rooted plants or trees that would compete with the rhubarb for water. As instructed, I dug in a barrel-load of well-rotted horse manure, although I knew there had already been a lot of it in the soil. "That rhubarb is going to be in the soil for an awfully long time," said Ged, encouraging me to provide a stockpile of nutrients in advance. As I planted the crown, I made sure the bud was kept well above ground, as it's prone to rot in the soil, and covered the roots completely.

I like to split and plant the crowns in autumn, but you can do it in early spring, too. Either way, it is critical you resist the temptation to harvest in the first year. If you do, you are likely to sabotage the plant's efforts to establish and end up with spindly, unattractive stalks. Let it grow and wilt in expectation of next year, covering the crown in organic matter during the dormant stage.

Force *Rhubarb*

Several gardening jobs are truly magical: earthing potatoes, which feels like finding treasure; noticing the first tomato fruits forming in mid-summer after you've nurtured the plant from seed for nearly half the year. None come close to the spellbinding experience of forcing rhubarb. It was discovered by accident in the 19th century, when one of the plants in a London botanical garden was inadvertently buried under the soil. Once excavated, the gardeners were amazed to find fresh growth of mesmerizing bright pink stems, which tasted far sweeter than the rhubarb grown outdoors...

By straining every sinew of its being to find the light, glucose, usually distributed between the rhubarb's large leaves and the stalks, remains in the stem. Forcing also allows for a much earlier harvest, remarkable for a crop ordinarily ready to harvest by the early spring months. During the Second World War, forced rhubarb became a national institution in the UK, its price regulated when fruit was scarce and rationed. The cultivation method is still prevalent in the "rhubarb triangle" of West Yorkshire. For centuries, the plants have been grown in large, dark forcing sheds, harvested, compellingly, in candlelight.

I, sadly, don't force my rhubarb in such a beguiling fashion. Still, the poignant tenderness of its bright stems never fails to move me, even in the dull February daylight. I cover my rhubarb as soon as I spot its buds emerging with their hopeful promise of spring. As a native to Serbia, rhubarb needs a short, sharp cold spell to awaken from dormancy, usually by the end of December or January. This is the best point to start eliminating light by covering it. I love the traditional terracotta forcers. They are beautiful and come with a little cap that allows for rot-deterring night ventilation, but can be pricey. As with anything else, I would encourage you to keep your eye out for a pre-loved one

rather than rushing to the garden centre – eBay is a reliable source, but you occasionally see them at antique markets and car boot sales (which are my go-to for old, steady, and often beautifully crafted gardening tools).

If you are not sure you would like to make that investment quite yet, a large dustbin (weighted down with bricks to prevent it from blowing away in the wind) will do the trick. Create a hole for ventilation, and pile manure heavy and thick around your forcer to release necessary warmth as it decomposes.

Allow the rhubarb to grow in the dark for 4–6 weeks before you try and harvest, aiming for long and slender bright pink stalks and acid yellow cabbage-like leaves. This early yield is only possible once you allow the plant to establish for at least three years before forcing, as any earlier than that, the extreme effort of trying to reach the light is likely to exhaust it. For the same reason, don't force the same plant for more than one year at a time. A year's rest is the minimum required for recovery. All the more reason to have a few rhubarb plants, of different varieties, that will allow you to rotate the forcer between them. For tips on harvesting rhubarb, see p112.

Growing in small spaces

In the soil, rhubarb can grow to an enormous size – it's not uncommon for most varieties to reach nearly 1.5m (5ft) in both height and width. Considering that, it is surprising that rhubarb is perfectly happy in containers, too. Granted, it won't get as large as its earthed peers, but a crown planted in, at least, a 40-litre (10-gallon) tub or pot will thrive as long as you fill it with excellent quality compost. I have been carrying a large pot of rhubarb between the gardens I have occupied as a city dweller in rented properties. As a hardy perennial that can take partial shade and is not disease-prone, it adjusts well to these transitions. I replenish its nutrients with mulch, a nitrogen-rich liquid feed, or by adding rotten manure to the soil and keep it regularly hydrated (plants that grow in pots always require more watering than the ones that can reach deep into the soil for moisture). I like to keep the pot amongst other grand perennials – irises and gladioli in my current set-up – which brings out the overlooked ornamental qualities of this beautiful plant.

Varieties

Ged told me that there are currently 11 varieties that grow well in his plot. There are many more out there, depending on your location and growing conditions. I stick to the following four, which give me a versatile and consistent harvest throughout the long growing season:

"Victoria" One of the oldest and most reliable varieties. Produces late, thick and juicy stalks. If you have struggled to get others to establish, try this one. It will reward you with armfuls of stems.

"Champagne" Early and elegant, with long delicate stalks in a pale hue that resembles pink champagne. Fantastic for forcing.

"Timperley Early" Bright red base fading into green in the early stages of the season – when it is at its best. Another excellent forcing variety (if you get into the habit, it's nice to have different types for rotation).

"Raspberry Red" As the name suggests, this rhubarb comes in a bright shade of nearly red pink. Grows early and tenderly, even without forcing.

Harvest *Rhubarb*

Unforced rhubarb is ready for harvest in the early spring – usually around late March to April, though a mild winter could push it into May. The length of the season will depend on the variety you have chosen to grow, but as long as you keep your rhubarb damp and the slugs away during crucial period of growth in early spring, it is likely to crop until mid-summer. The stems will be ready to harvest from the second growing year onwards when they are, ideally, 1–2.5cm (¹/₂–1in) in width and long, crisp and firm...

A common mistake (which I made, too) is to cut the base of the stem, which can lead to crown rot. Instead, pull the stalks with both hands and, with a gentle twist, yank them from the bottom of the plant. This will promote plant health and leave you with some crown residue (the brown tips that appear on the very end of the stalks), which is of great use for dyeing fabric alongside the toxic leaves (pp124–131).

Never pull more than one-third of the stalks at any given time, as a good amount of foliage is necessary for photosynthesis. Pick the stalks regularly – approximately every fortnight for younger plants, and every week for larger plants – but once the summer heat arrests the growth, rendering the stems flavourless, leave it to grow wild until it naturally dies when hit by the first frost.

Exhausted rhubarb tends to go to seed with the most dramatic, beady, cream flowers. As tempting as it is to keep these beauties intact, cut them back and keep them in a vase – they take vital energy from the plant. When dormant, split the crown if necessary (p109).

Rhubarb Kebabs

Serves 4

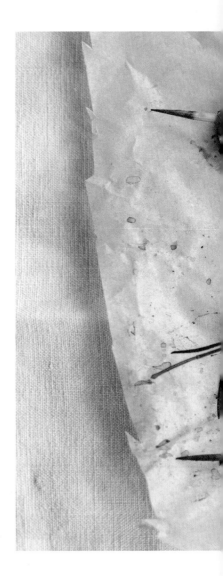

This may sound like the most uncanny combination but rhubarb is, in fact, used in meatballs and meaty stews in West Asian and Turkish cuisines. The provocative thing here, really, is taking the meat out of the equation. This recipe will also yield excellent falafels if you roll the mixture into balls, but there is something almost child-like and quintessentially summery in the pleasure of eating from skewers. If you're using wooden skewers, soak them in water for at least 10 minutes. I love making rosemary skewers – select long, strong sprigs and remove most of the leaves, leaving some at the top and bottom for decoration. These aromatic kebabs look and smell amazing on a barbecue – bake them in the oven for 15 minutes to set their shape before transferring to the grill.

Ingredients

360g/12¾oz/2 cups adzuki beans, soaked overnight, or 1 can adzuki beans (about 400g/14oz), drained

1 tsp sea salt

400g/14oz rhubarb, trimmed and chopped (save the leaves and browned crown edge for dyeing)

1 red onion, peeled, chopped and sautéed with 1 tbsp of olive oil for 7 minutes (save the skins for dyeing)

4 garlic cloves, peeled

4 tbsp olive oil

3 tbsp tahini

1 tsp vegan Worcestershire sauce or soy sauce

½ tsp liquid smoke (optional)

60g/2oz/scant ½ cup porridge oats, plus extra if needed

1 tbsp nutritional yeast

1 tsp ras el hanout spice mix

1 tsp ground cumin

½ tsp smoked paprika

½ tsp chilli flakes (optional)

20g/¾oz coriander leaves

selection of vegetables to add to the skewers, such as cherry tomatoes and chopped onions

Method

01 Drain the beans. In a large saucepan, cover the beans with 2 litres/3½ pints/8½ cups water. Add 1 tsp of salt, bring to the boil, reduce the heat to low, and cook for 30–60 minutes until the beans are soft, adding more water as needed. Drain and leave to cool.

02 In a food processor, blend the rhubarb until very finely chopped, but stop pulsing before it forms a paste. Add the beans, sautéed onion, garlic, oil, tahini, Worcestershire sauce, and liquid smoke. Process to a rough paste.

03 Add the oats, nutritional yeast, spices, coriander leaves, and remaining salt. Process lightly with a few sharp pulses, so the mixture is well combined but flecks of the coriander leaves still stand out. The mixture should be sticky but comfortable to handle. If it's too runny, add more oats.

04 Preheat the oven to 180°C/160°C fan/350°F/Gas 4. Wet your hands and carefully mould the mixture around the skewers (or roll into balls if you prefer falafel). You should have enough for 12–15 skewers if you keep the kebabs around 8cm/3¼in long. Add vegetables to the ends of each skewer as desired.

05 Bake for 30–40 minutes, until the kebabs form a crispy brown crust. If barbecuing, transfer to the barbecue grill after 15 minutes in the oven.

Rhubarb Dhal

Serves 6

Once your rhubarb plant establishes, you're likely to find it grows rampant. For that reason, I am always in the market for main, hearty rhubarb dishes, ones that can sustain you as a meal on their own, rather than yet another pudding – as delicious as they are! The idea of incorporating it in a dhal may seem unusual. Still, it is only an adapted version of the raw green mango dhal popular in India, where a sour, premature stage of the fruit grows in abundance. The tartness of the rhubarb is in no way overpowering here. As the rhubarb melts in the long cooking process, it provides more of a sharp backdrop to the earthy lentils, resulting in a substantial dish that is warming yet refreshing.

Ingredients

4 tbsp coconut oil

2 onions, peeled and chopped (save the skins for dyeing)

4 garlic cloves, peeled and finely chopped

5-cm/2-in piece of fresh ginger, peeled and finely chopped

1 red chilli, deseeded and finely chopped

1½ tsp cumin seeds, crushed

1 tsp coriander seeds, crushed

2 tsp sweet paprika

1½ tsp ground turmeric

1½ tsp khmeli suneli spice mix

1 small butternut squash, peeled and cut into 2-cm/¾-in chunks

250g/9oz rhubarb, trimmed and cut into 5-cm/2-in chunks (save the leaves and browned crown edge for dyeing)

2 red peppers, deseeded and diced

1 can chopped tomatoes (400g/14oz)

300g/10oz/1¾ cups red lentils

1.25 litres/2 pints/5 cups vegetable stock or water

1 tbsp chutney (I use mango)

4 tbsp date molasses

2 tbsp sea salt flakes, plus extra to season

freshly ground black pepper

chopped coriander, to serve

For the turmeric rice

1 tsp coconut oil

200g/7oz/1 cup brown rice

1 tsp ground turmeric

½ tsp sea salt flakes

For the tahini dressing

60g/2oz/¼ cup raw tahini

juice of ½ lime

pinch of ground cumin

Method

01 Melt the oil in a large saucepan over a medium-high heat. Lower the heat, add the onions, and cook for 5–7 minutes, until translucent. Stir in the garlic and cook for another minute before adding the ginger, chilli, and spices. Cook, stirring, for another minute until the onion and garlic mixture is coated and fragrant.

02 Add the butternut squash, rhubarb, and peppers and cook for 10 minutes. As the vegetables cook they will start to release their liquid, but add a little water if they start to stick to the bottom of the pan.

03 Add the tomatoes and lentils and mix well. Next add the stock, chutney, molasses, and salt and season with pepper. Stir well, bring to the boil, then simmer for about 40–50 minutes until the dhal has thickened to your liking.

04 Meanwhile, prepare the rice and the dressing. To make the rice, melt the oil in a medium pan over a medium-high heat, then lower the heat and add the rice, turmeric, and salt. Stir for 30 seconds until the rice is well coated, then add 500ml/16fl oz/2 cups of freshly boiled water. Bring to the boil, then cover and simmer for 30 minutes. Drain the rice and keep it covered in the pan.

05 To make the dressing, combine the tahini with the lime juice in a small bowl. Gradually add water, 1 tablespoon at a time, and whisk until the dressing has a fluffy, creamy consistency. Season with salt and pepper to taste and add a pinch of cumin.

06 Serve the dhal with the rice, a dollop of the dressing, and a sprinkle of chopped coriander.

Rhubarb and Lentil Kubbeh in Rhubarb and Squash Soup

Serves 6

There is no point pretending otherwise – this is a rather demanding recipe. Trust me, it's totally worth it! Kubbeh means "ball" in Arabic, and different versions of this soup and dumplings dish are popular in Iraqi, Kurdish, and Syrian cuisines. I like to make it on Christmas Eve, stuffing the dumplings with mushrooms and chestnuts. This version is the one I cook on the first Sunday that feels like spring, no matter what the calendar date is.

Ingredients

For the soup

3 tbsp rapeseed oil

2 red onions, peeled and chopped (save the skins for dyeing)

6 garlic cloves, peeled and finely chopped

400g/14oz rhubarb, trimmed and cut into pieces, each around 3–5cm/1¼–2in (save the leaves and browned crown edge for dyeing)

800g/1¾lb Crown Prince squash, pumpkin, or butternut squash, peeled and cut into pieces, each around 3–5cm/1¼–2in

½ can chopped tomatoes (200g/7oz)

3 cardamom pods, seeds ground to a powder

1 tsp cumin seeds, crushed

1 tsp coriander seeds, crushed

2 tsp baharat spice mix

1 tsp ground turmeric

2 tbsp vegan stock powder (optional)

4 tbsp pomegranate molasses

2 tbsp date molasses

2 tsp salt

2 tbsp nutritional yeast

For the dumplings

250g/9oz/1½ cups fine bulgur wheat

250g/9oz/1½ cups fine semolina

120g/4¼oz/1 cup tbsp plain flour

1 tsp sea salt

50ml/1¾fl oz/3½ tbsp rapeseed oil

For the stuffing

100g/3½oz/½ cup green lentils

200g/7oz rhubarb, trimmed and chopped

2 garlic cloves, peeled

3 tbsp tahini

1 tbsp olive oil

50g/1¾oz walnuts

20g/¾oz parsley, chopped, plus extra to serve

1 tsp khmeli suneli spice mix

grated zest and juice of ½ a lime

1 tsp sea salt

freshly ground black pepper

Method

01 Start with the soup. Heat the oil in a large saucepan over a medium-high heat. Lower the heat, add the onions, and cook for 5–7 minutes until translucent. Stir in the garlic and cook for 1 minute, then add the rhubarb and cook for 2 minutes, stirring occasionally.

02 Next add the squash, chopped tomatoes, and spices and mix well. Cover with 2.5 litres/4½ pints/10⅔ cups boiling water. Add the stock powder, if using. Bring to the boil. Add the molasses, salt, and nutritional yeast and reduce the heat. Simmer for 30 minutes.

03 Meanwhile, make the dumplings. In a large bowl, cover the bulgur in cold water and leave to soak for 15 minutes. Once absorbed, lightly separate the grains using your hands.

04 Add the semolina, flour, and salt and mix to combine. Add the oil and rub it in, using your hands (the texture should be lumpy at this stage). Gradually add 350ml–500ml/12–16fl oz/1½–2 cups lukewarm water, working in the liquid with your hands until you reach a soft, dough-like consistency.

05 To make the stuffing, cover the lentils in plenty of water in a medium pan. Bring to the boil and then simmer for 15 minutes. Drain and rinse under cold water. Put the lentils and the remaining stuffing ingredients in a food processor. Pulse the mixture until just combined and the texture is consistent.

06 Wet your hands and roll the dumpling dough into ping-pong-sized balls (you should get around 20–24). Wet your hands again and use your fingers to make a well in the centre of each ball. Fill the well with roughly 1 tablespoon of the stuffing and then gather the edges together to seal. This technique may seem tricky at first, but once you get used to forming the dumplings you'll get into a rhythm and it becomes second nature. Repeat until you've filled all the dumplings, wetting your hands repeatedly as you go.

07 Bring the soup to a boil and add the dumplings. Cook for 10–30 minutes, until the dumplings rise to the surface. Serve with a sprinkle of parsley.

Rhubarb, Celery, and Broad Bean Stew

Serves 6

I love the Persian kitchen but cannot deny it isn't the most vegan friendly of cuisines. This is a vegan version of khoresh karafs, a lamb and celery stew that I read about but never tasted, with a rhubarb twist. One of the things I love about the flavours of the region is the unapologetic use of tang – whether from Persian lime, fresh lime, pomegranate, or sumac. Rhubarb fits this framework perfectly and suits this dish, as I like to think of rhubarb as a long-lost relative of celery (though I know for a fact the two aren't related).

Ingredients

200g/7oz/1⅓ cups dried broad beans, soaked overnight in cold water, then drained

1 tsp sea salt

3 tbsp olive oil

2 onions, peeled and chopped (save the skins dyeing)

4 garlic cloves, peeled and finely chopped

1 tsp ground turmeric

200g/7oz celery sticks, cut into 3-cm/1¼-in chunks

250g/9oz rhubarb, trimmed and cut into 3-cm/1¼-in chunks (save the leaves and browned crown edge for dyeing)

1 tbsp vegan stock powder (optional)

20g/¾oz mint leaves, chopped

20g/¾oz parsley leaves, chopped, plus extra to serve

juice and zest of 1 lime

50ml/1¾fl oz/¼ cup date molasses

2 tbsp nutritional yeast

½ tsp ground cinnamon

½ tsp saffron strands (optional)

freshly ground black pepper

Turmeric Rice and Tahini Dressing, to serve (pp116–117)

Method

01 Place the beans in a large saucepan, then add 2 litres/3½ pints/8½ cups water and the salt. Bring to the boil, then reduce the heat and cook for 45 minutes, topping up the water as necessary. Drain.

02 Heat the oil in another large saucepan over a medium-high heat. Lower the heat, add the onions, and cook for 5–7 minutes, until translucent. Add the garlic and cook for another minute. Add the turmeric and stir until the onion and garlic are coated.

03 Add the celery, rhubarb, beans, and 750ml/1¼ pints/3¼ cups water and the stock powder, if using. Bring to the boil, then reduce the heat to low. Add the remaining ingredients and season with pepper.

04 Cook for 30 minutes, or until all the water evaporates and the vegetables and beans are slightly mushy. Serve hot, sprinkled with parsley, with Turmeric Rice and Tahini Dressing.

Rhubarb, Tahini, and Plum Crumble

Serves 4

An ode to my first ever rhubarb experience – the Food for Thought crumble. Only, as you may expect, the cooks of the legendary West End eatery never used tahini in their version. How did this condiment find its way into the humble crumble? It happened after Eyal Shani, one of my favourite Israeli chefs, made the connection. "Even lemon is incapable of connecting to tahini as well as rhubarb does", he wrote in one of his characteristically poetic food columns, which encouraged me to try and inject this Middle-Eastern staple into one of the most quintessential of English puddings. The result is a gooier crumble, with a texture that resembles a flapjack. Serve with a comforting splash of oat cream and a side of chutzpah.

Ingredients

250g/9oz plums, quartered and stones removed

450g/1lb rhubarb, cut into pieces, each about 2–3cm/¾–1¼in (save the leaves and browned crown edge for dyeing)

80g/2¾oz/⅓ cup golden caster sugar

¾ teaspoon ground cinnamon

½ teaspoon orange blossom water

½ teaspoon ground nutmeg

125g/4¼oz/1¼ cup rolled oats

100g/3½oz/1 cup ground almonds

60g/2oz/¼ cup raw tahini

zest and juice of ½ lime

oat cream or vegan vanilla ice cream, to serve

Method

01 Preheat the oven to 180°C/160°C fan/350°F/Gas 4.
Put the plums and rhubarb in a pie dish and toss them
in 1 tablespoon of the sugar, ¼ tsp of the cinnamon,
and the orange blossom water.

02 In a separate bowl, combine the remaining sugar and
cinnamon with the nutmeg, oats, and ground almonds.
Add the tahini, lime zest and juice to the dry
ingredients. Using your hands, rub the wet ingredients
into the dry until the mixture is well combined and
resembles breadcrumbs.

03 Layer the crumble over the fruit mixture and bake for
30–40 minutes until the top is golden and crispy.
Serve with oat cream or vegan ice cream.

Mordant with *Rhubarb*

Come spring, my plot is covered in loose rhubarb leaves. They coat the main path, lay trapped between large paving stones, and fill my wheelbarrow. These aren't the leaves of my rhubarb plants but my neighbours'. Since I told them that they are beneficial to my natural dye practice, they have provided me with more than I can handle. It isn't just their kindness (a common trait amongst gardeners, I find) but their enthusiasm for extracting value from an otherwise poisonous part of the plant that spurs this generosity.

Rhubarb leaves

Rhubarb leaves contain high levels of oxalic acid (a corrosive that can harm kidney function and cause a number of other health issues), which renders them unsuitable for human consumption yet perfectly safe for soil microorganisms. The leaves are often used as a weed-suppressing and water-retaining mulch around the rhubarb plant, yet many find their way to the compost heap (a practice I have to resort to at the height of the season, when the leaf donations overflow). I never think of anything that goes on the compost heap as "waste" – it is all part of nature's inspiring circle of life. Still, discovering I can extract a natural mordant from the leaves was a breakthrough moment.

Mordants, necessary to fix the dye colour to the fibre, are chiefly made of the metallic salts aluminium and iron and are the least natural component of the natural dye process. Similarly to oak galls (p22), rhubarb foliage contains a substantial amount of natural tannins. This makes rhubarb suitable for mordanting plant-based fabrics, such as cotton and linen – which I recommend for most of the garments in this book. However, the oxalic acid also makes a powerful mordant for animal fibres, such as silk and wool – so much so that 200g/7oz of rhubarb leaves can be used to mordant 1kg/2¼lb of fabric. For this reason, I have chosen to feature a silk organza version of the Rhubarb Bolero.

A note on animal fibres

While I decided to work with silk organza for the Rhubarb Bolero, this was not without caveats. The first is practical: animal fibres, silk mostly, and silk organza, in particular, are notoriously hard to cut and sew. If you don't have much experience, it can become demoralizing. The second is more philosophical: animal fibres, by definition, aren't vegan.

The best way to work with them (just as with plant-based fabric) is to upcycle. For the Rhubarb Bolero, I used organza taken from a damaged vintage prom-like dress I found in a charity shop. It required careful unpicking and cutting work to maintain the straight grain of the fabric, which is crucial in order to achieve the millimetre-precision needed when working with this shifty material.

Rhubarb leaf mordant

To make a rhubarb leaf mordant, you'll need at least 20g/³⁄₄oz of rhubarb leaves for every 100g/3½oz of fabric. Chop the leaves coarsely and place them in a large colander. If your skin is sensitive, wear gloves, as the oxalic acid may elicit an allergic reaction. I find that washing my hands, the knife, and the chopping board well immediately after is enough for me. Put the leaves in a deep pan and cover them with water. Bring to a boil and simmer for an hour over a very low heat. Allow to cool and then strain the liquid into another large pan. Add the rhubarb leaves to your compost heap.

Remember, the oxalic acid in the leaves can be poisonous so if you are working indoors, make sure the space is well ventilated – I open all the windows wide. I often work with a hot plate outdoors, weather permitting. On a hot summer's day, you can do the whole process outside without access to a heat source: cover the chopped leaves with freshly boiled water, and let them steep in the sun for 5–8 hours.

You don't have to use the mordant straight away. You could make it and keep it in an airtight jar in the refrigerator – it will store for up to a week in a non-sterile jar and up to 10 weeks in a sterile jar. Don't use it if it starts to smell rotten. Similarly, the fresh rhubarb leaves could be frozen to make a mordant in the winter months. In both cases, make sure to label the containers clearly, so you don't mistake their contents for a vegetable broth or swiss chard leaves.

Working with cotton and linen

If I want to mordant cotton or linen using rhubarb leaf mordant, I bind the fabric in plant-based milk first to boost its pigment-absorbing capabilities and use at least a 1:2 ratio of mordant to the fabric. To mordant the fabric, wet the cloth and submerge it in the strained solution in a deep pan (adding more water if needed to cover the fabric entirely). Simmer for 40 minutes, allow the vat to cool, then rinse the fabric (pp130–131).

Working with organza and silk

When mordanting silk organza or silk (or even wool yarn) with rhubarb leaf, there is no need to pre-bind the fabric before mordanting – the rhubarb leaf mordant is at its most potent when it comes into contact with animal fibre, so it doesn't require the extra boost that plant-based fibres do. You should use a 1:5–1:2 ratio of mordant to fabric (pp130–131).

Like many living organisms, rhubarb produces a natural toxin, oxalic acid. It's excellent for mordanting – but dangerous for human consumption.

Dye with *Rhubarb*

There is more than mordant in the rhubarb leaves – the natural tannins also add a yellow tint to the fibre and can be used in the vat as dyestuff in their own right.

Yellow shades

The mordanting process will leave your fibre with a vague yellow tinge. To build on that, increase your leaf to fabric ratio (take precautions due to the high concentration of oxalic acid in the leaves: increase the ventilation and wear a mask). Leaving the fabric to soak overnight or for up to 48 hours will yield a more vital

shade – vivid buttery yellows on plant-based fibres and yellowish khakis on animal fibres. Add vinegar to increase the vat's acidity towards the end of the soaking period for more mustardy hues.

As valuable as the leaves are, my favourite part of the plant is the crown when it comes to colour. As you can only obtain this dyestuff in the dormancy period, working with the rhubarb crown produces highly prized golden hues (though I have used Himalayan crown powders made of native species that produce deeper golden shades, which I buy from specialist retailers). To dye with the crown, you must split it into small pieces, which you'll need to do as soon as you can after harvesting it. Once it dries, it becomes hard as a stone. On the bright side, once cut and dried, this dyestuff can be stored in a brown bag for months, producing vivid dyes regardless of its age. The crown residue, the brown tips that appear on the very end of the stalks as you yank them, are an invaluable addition to the dye vat, too.

Pinks

At the height of the season, when the rhubarb is at its brightest, I even manage to extract some pink from the stalks themselves. (They produce a very mild dye – only obtainable for the fleeting time when the stalks are at their pinkest.) First, I bring the stalks to a boil and simmer before I add them to any of the recipes in the cook section. I then simmer the remaining liquid with the discarded bits of rhubarb left over from cooking. I may even add the broad bean cooking water in the case of the Rhubarb, Celery, and Broad Bean Stew (pp120–121). I once managed to dye a whole bolero this way, but I usually use this less reliable method to

dye small sections of fabric, such as the bolero's frilly panel or the tie.

A much more consistent (and completely magical) way to obtain pinky shades is using an alkaline modifier. To dye the pale rose colour of the shirt Ged is wearing opposite, I boiled and simmered a pre-sewn and alum-mordanted Blackberry Shirt with one cup of dried crown chunks. I let the shirt soak in the water for a whole night, and in the morning, I dissolved 5 tablespoons of soda crystals in a large pot of lukewarm water. Once I dipped the shirt in it, the wonderful alchemy of pH modification turned the light tan shade to pink. You can also reach shades of mauve or even light coral by increasing the dyestuff to fabric ratio.

Neutral hues

I love the warm golden tint of the upcycled organza Rhubarb Bolero (p132). It makes this garment look at once romantic yet sombre, perhaps reflecting the fact I made it at the end of a bittersweet love. I mordanted the pre-made bolero with rhubarb leaves and then dyed it with fresh rhubarb crown to reach this tone. When I tried to get this shade to work on cotton, I found that adding some black tea to the dye water helped achieve this deeper shade.

Working with the crown and an iron mordant (in a process in which it is added straight to the dye vat, with the fabric bound with plant milk in advance) helps to reach shades of grey, depending on the crown to iron mordant ratio: more mordant will get you to stone greys while less will keep things in the area of warm ecru (the Nettle Duster coat that Ged is sporting opposite was dyed in this very way). Work some of the rhubarb leaves into the dye vat alongside the crown pieces and the iron for a pale ochre.

See pages 18–23 for more detailed information on dyestuff, mordants, and dye vat ratios.

Rhubarb colour range

A Rhubarb Bolero could be anywhere between 35g–70g (1¼–2½ oz) in silk organza or cheesecloth to 120g (4oz) in medium-weight linen. These tentative dye "recipes" are for 100g (3½oz) of fabric – multiply the quantities as required and use enough water to cover the fabric. Bear in mind that the shade may vary depending on your fabric, water pH level, the time in the growing season, and serendipity.

Golden beige

Silk organza, mordanted with rhubarb leaves. Dyed with 75g (2½oz) of dried rhubarb crown chunks for every 100g (3½oz) of fabric. Boiled and simmered for 1 hours, left to steep for 4 hours.

Mellow peach

Lightweight cheesecloth bound with oat milk and mordanted with rhubarb leaves. Dyed with the cooking water drained from the beans in the Rhubarb, Celery and Broad Bean Stew (pp118–119). The infused water was used to simmer 250g (9oz) rhubarb stalks. To these, I added 40g (1½oz) of chopped rhubarb leaves and 60g (2oz) of rhubarb tips with crown resuide. Boiled for 1 hour, left to steep for 24 hours.

Buttery yellow

Medium-weight French linen, bound with oat milk. Dyed with 140g (5oz) chopped rhubarb leaves for every 100g (3½oz) of fabric. Boiled and simmered for 1 hour, left to steep for 48 hours.

Hazy coral

Medium-weight French linen, bound with oat milk and mordanted with rhubarb leaves. Dyed in an aluminium vat with 75g (2½oz) of dried rhubarb crown chunks, 40g (1½oz) of rhubarb tips with crown residue, and a pinch of grounded madder root for every 100g (3½oz) of fabric. Boiled and simmered for 3 hours, left to steep overnight, then dipped into a soda crystal bath made up of 1 tbsp of soda crystals to 1 litre (1¾ pints) of water for 5 minutes.

Rosy pink

Medium-weight antique linen, bound with oat milk and mordanted with alum. Dyed in an aluminium vat with 80g (2¾oz) of dried rhubarb crown chunks, and 50g (1¾oz) of rhubarb tips, with crown residue for every 100g (3½oz) of fabric. Boiled and simmered for 4 hours, left to steep overnight, then dipped into a soda crystal bath made up of 1 tbsp of soda crystals to 1 litre (1¾ pints) of water for 5 minutes.

Dusty pink

Medium-weight coarse antique linen, bound with oat milk and dyed with 50g (1¾oz) of dried rhubarb crown chunks for every 100g (3½oz) of fabric. Boiled and simmered for 2 hours, left to steep overnight, then dipped into a soda crystal bath made up of 1 tbsp of soda crystals to 1 litre (1¾ pints) of water for 5 minutes.

Pale ochre

Medium-weight antique linen mordanted with alum. Dyed with 70g (2¼ oz) of dried rhubarb crown chunks, 40g (1½oz) of chopped leaves, and 1 tbsp of iron-infused water for every 100g (3½oz) of fabric. Boiled and simmered for 2 hours, left to steep for 6 hours.

The Rhubarb Bolero

As I find rhubarb such an elegant crop, I wanted to make something a bit more evening-oriented. I think this cut looks ravishing in sheer fabrics, but don't feel compelled to work with organza unless you're an experienced sewer. A good alternative is cotton organdy, which looks like a papery, matt-finished organza. This fabric was a popular apron material in the early 20th century and the bolero pieces are pretty economical, so you could cut them from a few used aprons – plus the rhubarb dye is very good at concealing stains! The Rhubarb Bolero would also be beautiful cut from light linen or cotton voile, popular bases for many textile items ripe for upcycling.

Construction

Shown on the right are the pattern pieces for the Rhubarb Bolero (please see Pattern Sheet 1):

If you are working with a sheer fabric and feels confident with your sewing, try the French seam and pin hem options. But by no means consider the overlock and roll hem a cop-out – you could make these into a bold detail by using a contrasting thread colour.

All seam allowances are 1cm (⅜in) unless otherwise stated.

Measurements

Please refer to the appendix on p220 for size charts and fabric requirements. The primary measurements you need to consider here are the bust and waist.

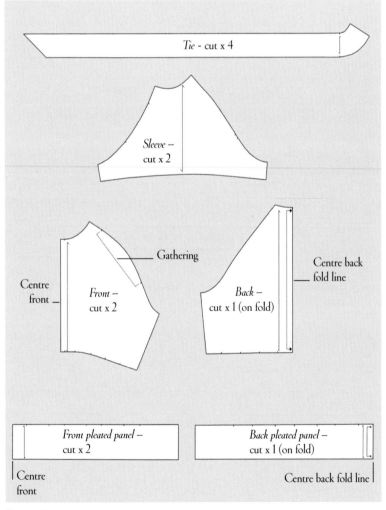

Tie - cut x 4

Sleeve – cut x 2

Centre front

Front – cut x 2

Gathering

Back – cut x 1 (on fold)

Centre back fold line

Front pleated panel – cut x 2

Back pleated panel – cut x 1 (on fold)

Centre front

Centre back fold line

Pattern pieces

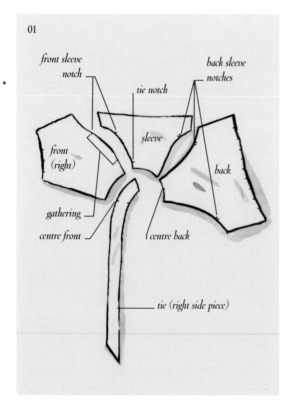

01

front sleeve
notch

back sleeve
notches

tie notch

sleeve

front
(right)

back

gathering

centre front

centre back

tie (right side piece)

01 **Familiarize yourself with the raglan
sleeve construction**

A raglan sleeve may look different from a traditional
one, but it is more straightforward to set in. The back
piece and sleeve are marked by two close notches, the
front piece by a single notch at the armhole. However,
the front piece also features notches that indicate the
start and end of the gathering line. The front sleeve
features another notch closer to the neckline, matching
the tie seam on the front piece.

The simplest way to attach the sleeves is to use an
overlock or zigzag stitch (see step 2). Alternatively, see
steps 3–5 for instructions on using a French seam; this
gives a more refined finish that is particularly good for
sheer or thin fabric.

02 **Attach the back piece to the back of the
raglan sleeves (overlock or zigzag finish)**

n the back and sleeve right sides together, matching the
notches. Sew, then press. Finish the seam allowances
together with an overlock or zigzag stitch. Repeat for
the other sleeve, then continue to step 6.

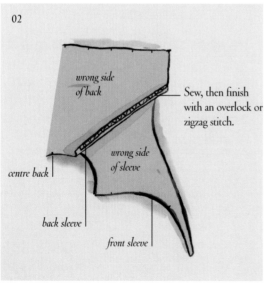

02

wrong side
of back

Sew, then finish
with an overlock or
zigzag stitch.

centre back

wrong side
of sleeve

back sleeve

front sleeve

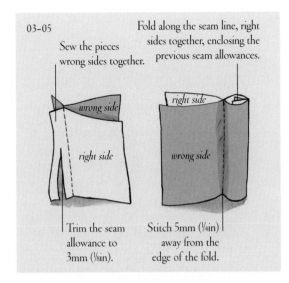

03-05

Sew the pieces wrong sides together.

Fold along the seam line, right sides together, enclosing the previous seam allowances.

right side

wrong side

right side

right side

wrong side

Trim the seam allowance to 3mm (⅛in).

Stitch 5mm (¼in) away from the edge of the fold.

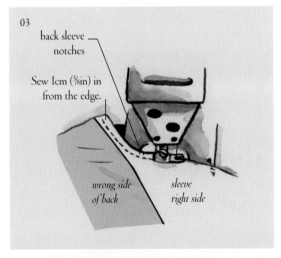

03

back sleeve notches

Sew 1cm (⅜in) in from the edge.

wrong side of back

sleeve right side

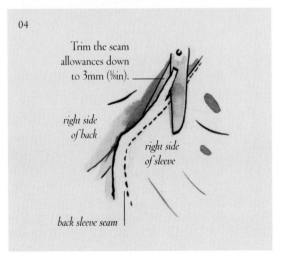

04

Trim the seam allowances down to 3mm (⅛in).

right side of back

right side of sleeve

back sleeve seam

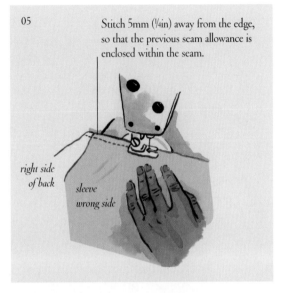

05

Stitch 5mm (¼in) away from the edge, so that the previous seam allowance is enclosed within the seam.

right side of back

sleeve wrong side

03 **Attach the back piece to the back of the raglan sleeves (French seam finish)**
Pin the back and sleeve wrong sides together and sew.

04 Trim both sides of the seam allowance down to 3mm (⅛in). Open the seam with the right side facing up, so that the seam allowance is on top. Press the seam allowances towards the sleeve.

05 Fold the fabric on the seam line, right sides are together. Stitch 5mm (¼in) away from the edge, so that the previous seam allowance is enclosed within the new seam. Press. Repeat steps 3–5 for the other sleeve.

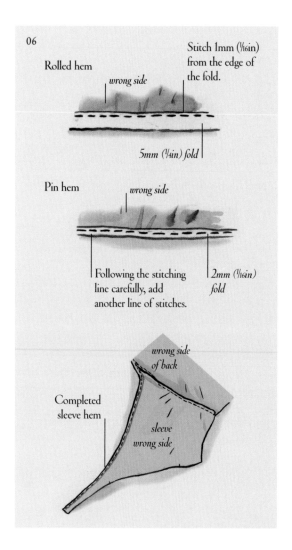

06

Rolled hem

wrong side

Stitch 1mm (¹⁄₁₆in) from the edge of the fold.

5mm (¼in) *fold*

Pin hem

wrong side

Following the stitching line carefully, add another line of stitches.

2mm (¹⁄₁₆in) *fold*

Completed sleeve hem

wrong side of back

sleeve wrong side

06 Stitch the sleeve hem

The simple option is a rolled hem:
a) Fold the sleeve hem to the wrong side by 5mm (¼in), press, then fold a further 5mm (¼in) and press again.
b) Stitch 1mm (¹⁄₁₆in) from the edge of the fold, using the inside edge of machine foot as a guide.
c) Press.
d) Repeat for the other sleeve.

For a more refined finish (for sheerer and thinner fabric), use a pin hem:
a) Fold the sleeve hem to the wrong side by 5mm (¼in) and press. Stitch 1mm (¹⁄₁₆in) away from the bottom edge.
b) Trim the seam allowance as close as possible to the stitching line.
c) Fold the fabric up 2mm (¹⁄₁₆in) above the stitching line, enclosing the raw edge, and add another line of stitches, following the first stitching line carefully.
d) Press.
e) Repeat for the other sleeve.

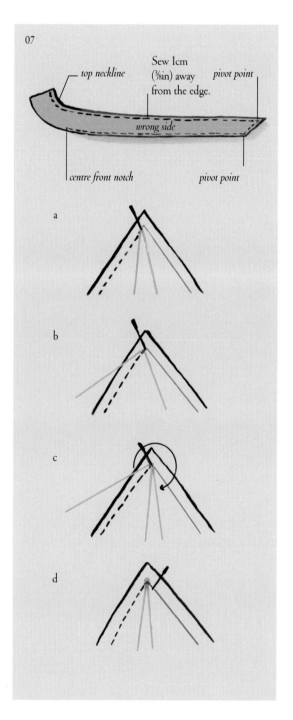

07

top neckline

Sew 1cm
(⅜in) away
from the edge.

pivot point

wrong side

centre front notch

pivot point

a

b

c

d

07 Sew the ties

Pin one pair of tie pieces right sides together, all the way up to the centre front notch. Start sewing from the top neckline. When you are one stitch away from the pivot point, keep your machine needle in the fabric, lift the presser foot and insert a length of doubled thread, wrapping it tightly against the needle (a). Lower the foot, then slowly make a single stitch over the thread (b). Leave the needle down and pull the thread on the right side over to the left, around the base of the needle, so that both lengths are pulled towards the bottom of the tie (c). Leave the needle down, and turn the tie ready to sew the next side. Pivot and sew a single stitch to "trap" the thread tail between the two stitches that make the corner (d). This hack will help you achieve a sharper corner. Repeat at the other corner and stitch all the way to the front notch seam.

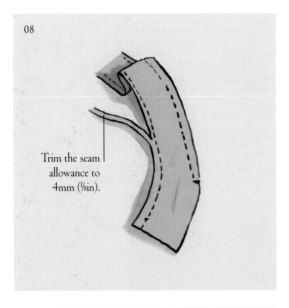

08

Trim the seam
allowance to
4mm (⅛in).

08 Trim the seam allowance down to 4mm (⅛in).

09 Using a pencil or loop turner, turn the tie right side
out. Insert the pencil or loop turner into the tie,
pushing it all the way down to the end seam, then pull
the right side of the fabric through so it is facing out.
Use the thread inserts to pull the corners out and then
cut off the threads. Repeat steps 7–9 for the other tie.

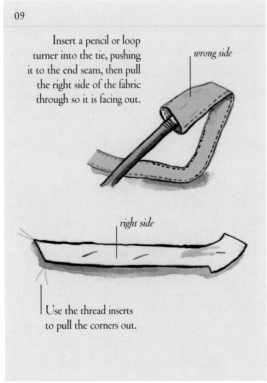

09

Insert a pencil or loop
turner into the tie, pushing
it to the end seam, then pull
the right side of the fabric
through so it is facing out.

wrong side

right side

Use the thread inserts
to pull the corners out.

10

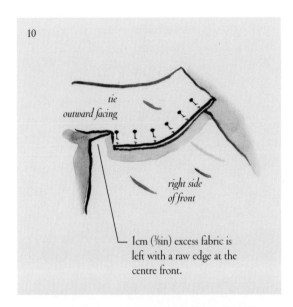

tie
outward facing

right side
of front

1cm (⅜in) excess fabric is
left with a raw edge at the
centre front.

12

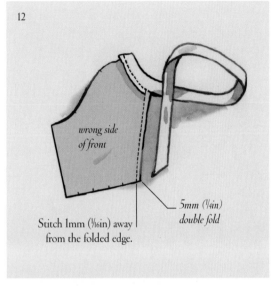

wrong side
of front

5mm (¼in)
double fold

Stitch 1mm (¹⁄₁₆in) away
from the folded edge.

11

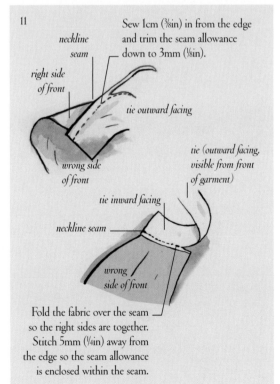

Sew 1cm (⅜in) in from the edge
and trim the seam allowance
down to 3mm (⅛in).

neckline
seam

right side
of front

tie outward facing

tie (outward facing,
visible from front
of garment)

wrong side
of front

tie inward facing

neckline seam

wrong
side of front

Fold the fabric over the seam
so the right sides are together.
Stitch 5mm (¼in) away from
the edge so the seam allowance
is enclosed within the seam.

10 **Attach the tie to the front piece**

Take one tie and one front piece. Matching the centre
front notches, pin the longer raw edge of the tie's
unstitched seam allowance to the centre front piece so
the wrong side of the front and the undertie are
together. There will be 1cm (⅜in) of excess fabric with
a raw edge at the centre front – this will later form the
front finish.

11 Repeat the French seam technique (see steps 3–5),
taking extra care with the curve. (You could opt for an
overlock or zigzag stitch here, but as this piece is close
to the neckline and may be visible when the bolero is
worn, it is well worth the effort that the French seam
technique requires.)

12 **Finish the centre front**

Fold the centre front line of the front to the wrong
side by 5mm (¼in), press, then fold again by another
5mm (¼in) and press. Stitch 1mm (¹⁄₁₆in) away from
the edge. Press. Repeat steps 7–12 for the other tie
and front piece.

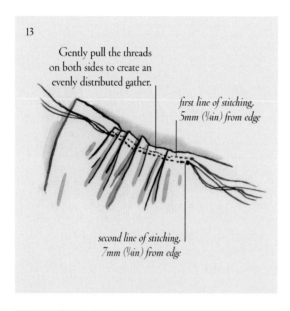

13

Gently pull the threads
on both sides to create an
evenly distributed gather.

*first line of stitching,
5mm (¼in) from edge*

*second line of stitching,
7mm (¼in) from edge*

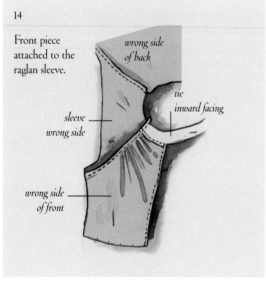

14

Front piece
attached to the
raglan sleeve.

*wrong side
of back*

*tie
inward facing*

*sleeve
wrong side*

*wrong side
of front*

13 **Gather the front raglan seams**

Adjust your machine stitch length to 4 and stitch two
lines between the gathering notches on the front piece
– the first 5mm (¼in) from the edge, and the second
7mm (¼in) from the edge. Don't reverse to reinforce
the stitches at the beginning and end, and leave plenty
of thread on each end. Gently pull the threads (only
from the top or only from the bottom of each stitch
line) to create an evenly distributed gathering. Match
to the measurement indicated on your pattern piece.
Repeat on the other front piece.

14 **Attach the front pieces to the raglan sleeves**

Pin and stitch the completed front piece to the front
sleeve line. If you are finishing with an overlock or
zigzag stitch, pin the pieces right sides together; if you
are opting for a French seam, pin the wrong sides
together and follow the instructions in steps 3–5.
Repeat for the other front piece and sleeve.

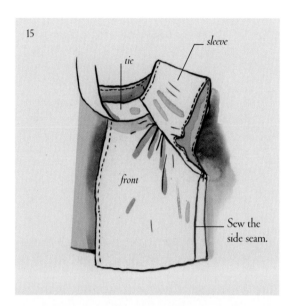

15

sleeve

tie

front

Sew the
side seam.

15 Sew the side seams

If you are finishing with an overlock or zigzag stitch,
pin the front and back right sides together along the
side seam and stitch; if you are opting for a French
seam, pin the panels wrong sides together and follow
the instructions in steps 3–5. Repeat for the other side.

16 Finish the back of the neckline

Cut 3mm (⅛in) long notches into the curviest part of
the neckline to alleviate the tension. Fold the neckline
to the wrong side by 5mm (¼in) in and then another
5mm (¼in), pressing with your fingers as you go along
to keep the folds in place. Topstitch around the
neckline 1mm (¹⁄₁₆in) away from the folded edge. Press.

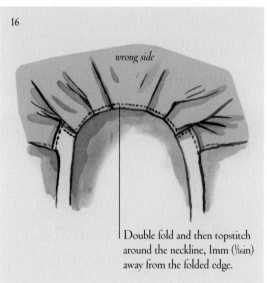

16

wrong side

Double fold and then topstitch
around the neckline, 1mm (¹⁄₁₆in)
away from the folded edge.

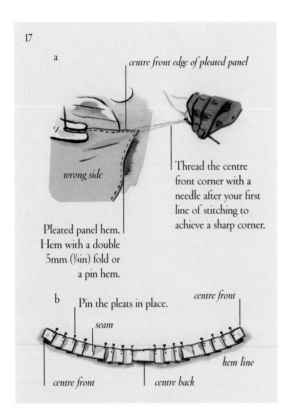

17

a

centre front edge of pleated panel

wrong side

Thread the centre
front corner with a
needle after your first
line of stitching to
achieve a sharp corner.

Pleated panel hem.
Hem with a double
5mm (¼in) fold or
a pin hem.

b Pin the pleats in place.

centre front

seam

hem line

centre front

centre back

17 Sew the pleated panel

Pin one front pleated panel to each short end of the
back pleated panel, making sure the centre front edge
of each front panel is the one that's left loose. Sew
together to form a long strip. If you are finishing with
an overlock or zigzag stitch, pin the panels right sides
together; if you are opting for a French seam, pin the
wrong sides together and follow the instructions in
steps 3–5.

Then, stitch the hem line, stitching from the top of one
short side, along the long edge, and up the other short
side. The most elegant finish is a pin hem (see step 6).
If you opt for a pin hem, thread the centre front corner
with a needle after your first line of stitching, to keep
the corner sharp as you pivot (a). Alternatively, fold in
5mm (¼in) and then another 5mm (¼in) to the wrong
side of the fabric, then topstitch 1mm (¹⁄₁₆in) away from
the fold. Press. Pin the pleats according to the notches
on the pattern (b). Tack across the pleats to hold them
in place, then remove the pins.

18 Attach the pleated panel to the bolero

Pin the pleated panel to the body of the bolero,
matching the notches. Stitch in place, then finish
with an overlock or zigzag stitch, or use a French
seam (see steps 3–5). Press all over.

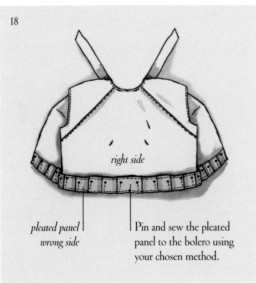

18

right side

*pleated panel
wrong side*

Pin and sew the pleated
panel to the bolero using
your chosen method.

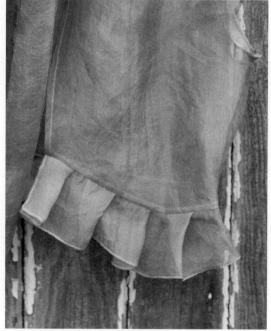

Blackberry

Every year, come late summer, blackberry picking becomes something of a competitive sport in my neighbourhood. Families come out with stepladders and fill enormous containers with the dark, sweet fruit while gobbling a fair amount as they go. The marshlands, and the roads leading to them, are absolutely jam-packed with blackberry brambles so, luckily, there is plenty of fruit to go around. This ubiquity points to why you might want to be careful with blackberry in your garden: it can be an incredibly invasive plant, and you may already be able to enjoy fresh berries not far from your doorstep. Even so, there are still some excellent reasons to introduce a blackberry shrub to your growing area. For one, cultivated blackberries tend to grow bigger, sweeter and are more succulent than their wild counterparts. The promise of a pain-free harvest, provided by domesticated thornless varieties, is also enticing. Grown on a trellis, blackberry can be used to create a natural barrier or fence to provide privacy. Despite being a low-maintenance plant, it will reward you with plenty of delicious fruit every year and act as a wildlife sanctuary in your backyard. It will also produce a wide arc of colours, from vibrant summer hues to more sombre autumnal shades, symbolic of the beautiful seasonal transition that occurs during their harvest period.

Cultivate *Blackberry*

"Blackberry first," said Mr Sadiq when he volunteered to help me clear the overgrown plot I'd taken earlier that winter. I was a little puzzled. I love blackberries, whether I'm eating them or adding them to a dye vat, so I wasn't sure why the dormant canes at the back were such a priority. To me, it seemed more urgent to tackle the intensely overgrown front, which I was more eager to cultivate. If the wild blackberries stayed there for the summer, I thought, they would at least repay me with a nice harvest, which is more than I could say about the endless layers of couch grass I was battling...

This goes to show how little I knew about good husbandry back then. Now when I routinely pluck out the fresh wild blackberry seedlings that surface throughout the growing season, I think about that little row I had with Mr Sadiq and it makes me laugh – though I can still see the logic in my initial argument. I changed my mind as soon as he started digging and exposed their deep and robust rootstock, which to my eye resembled a cardiovascular system, complete with a heart-shaped core.

Brambles, the thorny, bowed canes that host the wild blackberry, are some of the most vigorous and invasive perennials you will encounter. So although it may sound paradoxical, my main advice when it comes to growing your own is first to remove the wild bramble that is more likely than not already growing in your garden, particularly if your planting space is limited.

It's unlikely that you'll eradicate wild brambles completely – you will have to keep them in check. It can be tedious, like any old weeding job, but there is an upside: their presence will show you which part of your soil is most suitable for more manageable blackberry cultivation. They like free-draining yet moisture-retentive ground, such as fertile, light clay soils, which are relatively common in urban gardens.

They can take partial shade, but reward you with a more bountiful harvest when grown in full sun. Another important factor is choosing a spot that can accommodate a good support structure. Unless you're considering a dwarf cultivar (which are fantastic for small spaces and even do well in pots), their lanky canes require a sturdy backing, one that could be offered by a fence, wall, trellis, or a well-anchored wire system.

An enchanting backdrop

With some good planning, blackberries trained to grow over a structure can become an attractive feature in your outdoor space. They can even be used as an environmentally friendly screen – particularly in small, neighbour-surrounded gardens or on a busy street-facing balcony. One of the loveliest garden layouts I've ever encountered had a large living fence of evergreen thornless blackberries, which secluded a patio at the rear of a garden in a densely populated terraced street. The plants offered some privacy from the neighbouring backyards and created an enchanting backdrop for this hidden dining area.

The foliage changed throughout the year, with the gentle buds forming in late April, followed by the delicate blossom in May. Come late summer, it was covered in clouds of fruit at various stages of ripening: pale green, mauve, scarlet red, and deep, glossy purple. The owners once told me they regretted planting them, after realizing that the house was surrounded by wild brambles that would satisfy their blackberry cravings. But to me, what they achieved wasn't about the fruit, as delicious as it is: they managed to create a habitat for wildlife, a secret oasis, with the most modest of means.

Propagation and care

I say modest means, as it doesn't take much to propagate blackberry cuttings. It is wise to start with a nursery-propagated plant – select a variety that's suitable for your space. Once it has established, you can easily grow more by mimicking how brambles reproduce in nature. If you have ever been out foraging for blackberries, you will be familiar with the way their branches arch, forming a sort

of natural barbed-wire barrier. Everything in nature happens for a reason and my initial assumption was that this structure was the plant's way of protecting itself from predators. But it's actually a survival mechanism to make the plant prolific: bowing towards the soil, the plant sends down its freshest shoots, which take root as they touch the ground.

To replicate this technique, cut the top 15cm (6in) of one of the leafiest and firm canes on your plant. Place the tip 5cm (2in) deep in moist, fertile soil, or pot with good-quality, peat-free compost. Keep perpetually moist during the first month as the plant develops a new root system. The best periods for propagating are the same as they are for new shrub planting: during the autumn or spring.

Whether grown from a cutting or a garden-ready plant, blackberries fruit on two-year-old canes. It may seem brutal, but the best thing to do in the first year you grow them is cut them to the bud, encouraging healthier growth in the following spring. From that point onwards, you will be repeating the most essential of blackberry maintenance jobs – tying and pruning. Cut down canes to soil level after they have fruited and tie new canes to your support structure as they emerge in spring. In areas prone to hard frost, tie all the canes together. Reliable as they are, you will be able to quickly train them into place come spring, while keeping them from taking over your garden.

Forage and Harvest *Blackberry*

The wonderful thing about blackberries is that you don't have to grow them yourself to enjoy their fresh luscious fruit or the joy of picking them. Abundant in North America and Europe, wild blackberry foraging is woven into many "last days of summer" tales. I still get awfully excited about blackberry picking, despite the fact that I grow some cultivated varieties, too. A big part of the thrill is spotting the first ones that ripen, shining dark amongst the vicious thorns...

I can never quite resist the temptation to pick the first seemingly mature fruit I come across, but more often than not they are still too stiff and sharp. It's never a surprise, as blackberries have their way of letting you know when they are in their prime. Once they're ready to harvest, cultivated or wild, they will give in with just a gentle tug. (If you have to use any pressure at all to remove them from the plant, you will be disappointed once they reach your taste buds.) You get a feel for this quickly once you start foraging, and you should hold on to it year after year, as it's the best way to assure a pleasingly sweet bounty. As our weather patterns change, the height of the blackberry season and its length also shifts. You mustn't rely on the traditional period of August to early October. Last year, I picked the best fruits in July. This year, after an alternation of (rather cold) dry spells and unprecedented downpours, most were still sour in late August and many had shrivelled by the second week of September.

The sight of any fruit rotting unpicked is dour, but as you expand your foraging focus from wild food to dye plants, you start to learn to recognize the potential of fermented and dried berries. They are as beneficial to your dye vat as the pigment you can extract from the fresh fruit you would use for the following recipes, even if

they may provide less vibrant shades as they darken and harden. For that reason, I always carry two containers when I am picking: one for the fresh berries I can cook with and another for anything else. The second category contains anything that in pre-dyeing days I would have left on the shrubs or discarded, deeming them unsuitable for eating due to pest and rot damage.

You often find that blackberries and nettles grow side by side. In fact, as foraging urban legends tell, the sweetest berries are the ones that nestle amongst clumps of the common stinger. Some pickers view it as a (quite literal) pain, but it's something I am grateful for, as I often forage both within the same session. However, I tend to get caught out, particularly on warmer, late summer days, when I tell myself I'll be fine in my Onion Dress (p54) and a pair of clogs if I'm careful enough. If you are not as blasé as I am about the occasional prick of nettle or bramble thorn, the most sensible advice I can give you is to cover up for these double foraging affairs. Glove up, keep your calves out of harm's way, and cover your arms. The Blackberry Shirt(dress) will provide you with the latter while also allowing you to pick worry free: any strikes of the burgundy juice will blend in harmoniously, whether you choose to dye it before or after your foraging session.

....

Reliable thornless varieties

"Loch Ness" – A heavy cropper with dark, large fruit that will keep on providing until the first frost. Does well in large containers, but has the potential to reach 2m (7ft) in height when planted in open soil.

"Navaho" – A rather early variety with upright canes and large beautiful blooms, which are loved by pollinators. Ideally grown in open ground, but will tolerate 40-litre (10-gallon) containers.

"Opal" – A productive dwarf variety that will happily grow in pots and will suit small gardens, balconies, or patios.

....

Aubergine, Lentil, Blackberry, and Walnut Stew

Serves 6

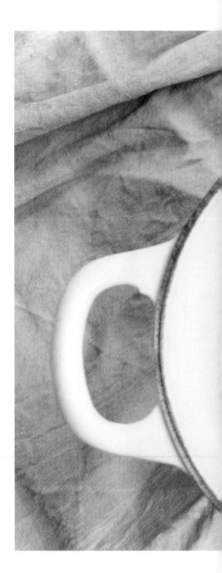

This is my version of fesenjān, a Persian stew with a walnut and pomegranate sauce. It is a traditional feature of the Chelleh Night festival – the celebration of the winter solstice. I never tasted the original meaty version, but I can just imagine how this rich, velvety stew is the most soothingly warm thing one could consume on the longest and darkest night of the year. Blackberries fill the opulent shoes of the pomegranate as the star of this dish, giving it deep and complex sweetness and colour. Their texture also adds a beautiful contrast to the crumbly walnuts and the melt-in-your-mouth consistency that the aubergine develops.

Ingredients

300g/10oz/2⅓ cups blackberries
2 aubergines, diced
3tsp sea salt
8 garlic cloves, peeled and finely chopped
4 tbsp olive oil
250g/9oz/1½ cups brown lentils
3 tbsp pomegranate molasses
2 tbsp date molasses
1 tbsp ground cumin
1 tsp khmeli suneli spice mix
1 tsp ground cinnamon

½ tsp hot paprika
4 bay leaves
juice of 1 lime
20g/¾oz coriander leaves, chopped, plus extra to serve
20g/¾oz mint leaves, chopped
150g/5½oz walnuts, chopped
freshly ground black pepper
tumeric rice and tahini dressing, to serve (p116–117)

Method

01 Put the blackberries in a pan and cover with water. Bring to the boil, then reduce the heat and simmer gently for 5 minutes. Strain and leave the berries to cool (save the cooking water for the blackberry dye, p160).

02 In a large saucepan, cover the aubergine with water and add 1 teaspoon of salt. Bring to the boil, then reduce the heat to medium-low and simmer for 10–15 minutes, until the aubergine softens.

03 Add the garlic and oil and stir until combined. Then add the softened blackberries, lentils, molasses, spices, bay leaves, and lime juice. Stir to combine and bring to a simmer. Then reduce the heat to low and continue cooking for 30 minutes, or until thickened and fragrant. Stir occasionally and add a splash of water if the stew gets too dry.

04 Stir in the coriander, mint, walnuts, and remaining salt and season with pepper to taste. Cook for at least another 5 minutes (much like dhal, the longer you cook it, the more mushy and comforting it will become).

05 Remove the bay leaves and serve warm with turmeric rice and tahini dressing (pp116–117).

Blackberry, Rosemary, and Peanut Focaccia

Makes 1 large focaccia

I've been told that this bread tastes like brioche. As vegan baked goods go, it's a lovely compliment, but that wasn't my intention. What I really wanted to achieve with this focaccia was a grown-up interpretation of my favourite breakfast treat – a peanut butter and jam sandwich – that I wouldn't feel bad about serving (and eating!) at a dinner party. While there is no need to expound on the frivolous joy of combining berries and peanuts, pairing blackberry and rosemary is a less obvious but equally pleasing partnership. Rosemary isn't the only herb that complements this dark fruit – thyme, sage, or oregano leaves would also provide a sophisticated twist to this moreish bread.

Ingredients

200g/7oz/1½ cups blackberries

500g/1lb 2oz/3½ cups strong white bread flour,
  plus extra for dusting

1 tbsp dried active yeast

1½ tsp sea salt flakes, plus extra for sprinkling

3 tbsp light muscovado sugar

4 tbsp olive oil, plus extra for oiling and drizzling

75g/2½oz/½ cup roasted peanuts, halved

4 sprigs of rosemary, leaves picked

Method

01 Put the blackberries in a pan and cover with water. Bring to the boil, then reduce the heat and simmer gently for 5 minutes. Strain and leave the berries to cool (save the cooking water for the blackberry dye, p160).

02 In a large mixing bowl, combine the flour, yeast, salt, and sugar. Mix well, then add the oil and 350ml/12fl oz/1½ cups lukewarm water. Using your hands, combine the ingredients and knead for 7 minutes in the bowl. The dough should be pretty sticky to start with, but will become more cohesive and softer as you go. Transfer to a well-oiled bowl and cover with a damp tea towel. Leave to rise for 1–1½ hours, or until the dough has doubled in size.

03 Once the dough has risen, dust your work surface lightly with flour. Tip the prepared dough out of the bowl and roll it into a ball. Leave to rise for a further 20 minutes.

04 Preheat the oven to 220°C/200°C fan/425°F/Gas 7 and line a large baking tray with baking paper. Roll the dough into a rectangle, roughly 32 x 23cm/12½ x 9in, and transfer it to the lined tray. Decorate with the softened blackberries (slightly pushing them into the dough) and sprinkle with peanuts, rosemary leaves, and salt to taste.

05 Drizzle with oil and bake for 20–25 minutes, or until the top is golden and the bottom golden-brown. Serve warm or at room temperature.

Lentil, Blackberry, and Cucumber Salad

Serves 6

This is, by far, the recipe I've been asked to share the most – it always stuns me. I never know if it's because I make it so often (which gives it plenty of opportunities to be appreciated) or because it is, in fact, one of my most compelling dishes (which might be why I choose to make it so frequently in the first place). What I do know is that it's straightforward to make and packed with lovely flavours and textures disproportionate to the minimal time and effort it requires. It's a perfect dish for a no-fuss, late summer lunch when the blackberry season is just starting. Their succulent texture complements the lentils so well and the secret ingredient, ground cinnamon, intensifies their flavour. When the berries are out of season, I increase the amount of currants to around 40g–65g/1½–2¼oz/⅓–½ cup for extra sweetness.

Ingredients

300g/10oz/1½ cups Puy or green lentils
150g/5½oz/1 cup blackberries
1 large cucumber, chopped
1 red onion, peeled and finely chopped
  (save the skin dyeing)
3 tbsp currants
20g/¾oz parsley leaves, chopped
20g/¾oz mint leaves, chopped
1½ tsp ground cinnamon
½ tsp chilli flakes (optional)

3 tbsp olive oil
2 tbsp balsamic vinegar
2 tsp sea salt
freshly ground black pepper
Tahini Dressing, to serve
  (p116–117)

Method

01 Put the lentils in a large saucepan and cover with cold water. Don't add salt to the cooking water, as it will make the lentils mushy.

02 Bring to a boil, then reduce the heat to medium and simmer for 15–20 minutes until the lentils are cooked but still have a bit of a bite. Drain in a colander, then rinse the lentils under cold water.

03 Transfer the lentils to a large bowl, then add all of the remaining ingredients and mix well. Season with pepper to taste. Serve the salad at room temperature or chilled, drizzled with Tahini Dressing.

Oat Milk and Blackberry Clafoutis

Serves 6 to 8

This is one of my favourite puddings. I'm still not entirely sure
I pronounce it correctly and, anyway, it never sounds as good
as when my French friend Sonia utters it with glee. She was stunned
to find that this pudding, essentially an eggy flan, could be veganized.
It was possible due to two revelations. The first was that aquafaba (the
liquid drained from organic tinned chickpeas or surplus chickpea
cooking water) can be foamed like egg white and used as a vegan
binder. The second was the creamy consistency of the new generation,
full-fat oat milk, developed initially to help baristas froth plant-based
flat whites. I personally can't stand it in coffee, but it has helped me up
my vegan baking game to a whole new level.

Ingredients

225g/8oz/1¾ cups blackberries
100ml/3½fl oz/scant ½ cup aquafaba
  (the liquid from a tin of chickpeas)
5 tbsp golden caster sugar
3 tbsp vegan butter, melted, plus extra for greasing
60g/2oz/scant ½ cup plain flour
225ml/8fl oz/scant 1 cup full-fat or
  "barista" oat milk
1 tsp vanilla extract
zest of ½ lemon
pinch of fine sea salt
1 tbsp maple syrup

Method

01 Put the blackberries in a pan and cover with water. Bring to the boil, then reduce the heat and simmer gently for 5 minutes. Strain and leave the berries to cool (save the cooking water for the blackberry dye, p160).

02 Preheat the oven to 185°C/165°C fan/365°F/Gas 4½ and grease a 24-cm/9½-in round pie dish with butter.

03 In a large bowl, whisk the aquafaba with the sugar for 2–3 minutes until thick and foamy.

04 Stir in the melted butter. Add the flour and whisk until smooth, then slowly stir in the oat milk, vanilla extract, lemon zest, and salt.

05 Pour half the batter into your prepared dish and bake for 15 minutes.

06 Remove from the oven. Carefully arrange the softened blackberries over the partially set batter (bear in mind that the dish will be very hot!) and drizzle with the maple syrup.

07 Give the remaining batter a stir and pour it over the blackberry layer. Return the dish to the oven and cook for another 35–45 minutes until the top is golden and the edges have browned. Leave to cool completely to allow the clafoutis to set, then slice and serve.

Blackberry and Cardamom Maqluba

Serves 10 to 12

No one marries Italian and British quite as well as Nigella Lawson. This is a vegan ode – with a Middle-Eastern twist – to her Anglo-Italian Rice Pudding Cake, which appears in her book *Cook, Eat, Repeat*. Maqluba literally means "upside down" in Arabic. In culinary terms, it is a savoury (often meaty) rice-based dish, a popular all-in-one meal in Palestinian, Syrian, Jordanian, and Iraqi cuisines. In transitioning it into a pudding, I brought in some of the ingredients synonymous with the desserts of these regions – pistachios and cardamom. Both complement the blackberries beautifully, underpinning them with stunning depth. Another Middle-Eastern staple, tahini, helps keep the rice mixture together while adding a lovely hint of halva-esque nuttiness.

Ingredients

400g/14oz/3 cups blackberries

1½ tsp coconut oil or vegan butter

300g/10oz/heaped 1½ cups pudding rice

1.5 litres/2¾ pints/6¼ cups oat milk

½ tsp fine sea salt

zest and juice of 1 lemon

90g/3¼oz vegan butter, plus extra for greasing

4 tbsp raw tahini

100g/3½oz/½ cup + 3 tbsp golden caster sugar

6 cardamom pods, crushed and seeds removed

125ml/4½ fl oz/½ cup aquafaba (the liquid from a tin of chickpeas)

¼ tsp grated nutmeg

100g/3½oz/¾ cup pistachio kernels, chopped, plus extra to serve

2 tsp orange blossom water

1 tsp ground cinnamon

Method

01 Put the blackberries in a pan and cover with water. Bring to the boil, then reduce the heat and simmer gently for 5 minutes. Strain and leave the berries to cool (save the cooking water for the blackberry dye, p160).

02 Melt the coconut oil in a medium saucepan. Add the rice and stir for 30 seconds until thoroughly coated. Add the oat milk, salt, and lemon zest and bring to a simmer, then turn the heat to low. Cook very gently, stirring occasionally, for 35–45 minutes, or until most of the milk has been absorbed. Transfer to a large bowl, stir in the vegan butter and tahini, and mix until combined.

03 Meanwhile, prepare the blackberry and cardamom layer. Combine the blackberries, half of the lemon juice, 3 tablespoons of the sugar, and half of the cardamom seeds in a small saucepan. Heat gently for 4–6 minutes – the mixture should resemble a thick compote with the blackberries largely holding their shape. Remove from the heat and leave to cool.

04 Preheat the oven to 170°C/150°C fan/325°F/Gas 3–4 and grease a 26-cm/10-in round springform cake tin with vegan butter. Spread the blackberry mixture in an even layer across the bottom of the tin.

05 In a small bowl, whisk together the aquafaba and the remaining sugar until thick and foamy, then fold into the rice mixture. Add the remaining lemon juice and cardamom seeds, nutmeg, pistachios, orange blossom water, and cinnamon and mix with a wooden spoon to combine.

06 Using a spatula, carefully spread the rice mixture over the blackberry layer, then gently smooth the surface. Bake for 45–55 minutes until the top is golden and the cake doesn't feel too wobbly (it will firm up completely as it cools). Remove from the oven and leave to cool in the tin.

07 Once at room temperature, unclip the spring and turn the tin onto a plate with the bottom side up. Run a butter knife around the inside of the tin base, to separate it from the sticky blackberry layer, and carefully remove it from the cake. Sprinkle with pistachios and serve.

Dye with *Blackberry*

Blackberry season epitomizes the most beautiful and fleeting transition – the moment that summer gives way and autumn begins. Therefore, it isn't surprising that the act of blackberry picking has been featured heavily in poetry and prose, metaphorically employed by the likes of Sylvia Plath, Yusef Komunyakaa, and Margaret Atwood. My personal favourite is the poem carrying this exact title – "Blackberry-Picking" by Seamus Heaney. It's a classic often taught in literature classes in school. Here, the ripening of the fruit symbolizes the coming of age, the loss of innocence. "Like thickened wine: summer's blood was in it" is the line that stayed with me after I first read it. I think of it every time I pick and, particularly, when I dye with blackberries.

Blackberries can create shades that are burning with heat, that evoke the exuberance and frivolity of summer; they can also produce some profoundly melancholic and complex hues. Summer's blood is indeed in them.

Dynamic beauty

This versatility – and the emotional impact of the shades it produces that never fails to move me – is why I love dyeing with blackberry. The secondary reason for it being one of my all-time favourite natural dyes is the much-appreciated, zero-waste aspects you discover once you start using it as a dye plant. Shrivelled and fermented berries, whether they are still lurking on the

canes or pressed against the bottom of your foraging container, can make a vital addition to the dye vat. The ones that are over-ripe, their sweet flesh suddenly turned sour, are beneficial for extracting the more dynamic, vivid hues, while the dried, crumbling berries make for a more dusky, sombre vat. The berries aren't the only part of the plant that have value beyond their natural life cycle: the leaves and fruiting canes are also a source of beautiful colours. In fact, their addition is what makes this plant such a wonderfully versatile dyestuff. I always use the canes and the leaves after the plant has fruited, as this is when you will have to prune them anyway to maintain its health. This task is sometimes also performed by trusts that manage woodlands, marshes, and parks, in an effort to keep the invasive brambles from taking over paths. If you have permission, you could pick the canes and leaves from the piles left behind to dry.

Preparing the dye vat

Prolific in the wild – and bearing in mind I can also use the less appetizing, over-ripe fruit – the garment I designed for this dye is a shirt(dress), as the style of its

longer variation, naturally, requires more dyestuff. For this, I like to use the cooking water I obtain from preparing the blackberries for somw of the recipes in this book, as the base of my dye (pp150–159).

To this blackberry-tainted water (which smells delicious and bears an equally luscious colour), I add my dried or fermented blackberries, which I crush a little to help them release more pigment. I bring them to the boil and then simmer for 30 minutes on a gentle heat. I strain the water well before I add the fabric – unless I am happy for it to have an uneven, micro polka-dot pattern, which emerges as the disintegrated drupelets strike the cloth.

When I want to add leaves and canes, they need to be chopped before they're added to the vat – remember to wear protective gloves if you are dealing with thorny ones. Leafy bramble shoots that you'd weed regularly from your garden may also be added to this vat, making the task of pulling their piercing seedlings less agonizing. When adding leaves, canes, or shoots, bring the dye vat to the boil, reduce the heat to low, and simmer for 45 minutes, then strain before adding your fabric.

Vivid hues

It may come as a surprise, but the "summer" end of the blackberry dye spectrum is mainly produced by steeping your fabric in a dye vat prepared with thorny canes and shoots. When mixed with blackberry or woad leaves, they can make sunny yellows, bright yellowish khakis that look like sun-kissed grass, and vibrant green shades.

I'm never particularly eager to use copper sulphate powder as a mordant, despite the beautiful colour it can yield, as it's toxic (p22). But I do feel comfortable using copper-infused water as an incidental modifier, particularly when it comes to dyeing with brambles, as they respond particularly well to this experimental ingredient. I drop 100ml/3½fl oz/scant ½ cup of homemade copper solution into the vat, alongside the plant material, and simmer. This helps achieve some orangey hues, such as rusty corals and burnt amber tones.

A very concentrated vat of over-ripe fruit will yield slightly dirty magenta tones, which can shift towards cerise with the addition of some citric acid modifier.

Dusky shades

To me, the most beloved hues I can extract from blackberries are the purples you find in the autumn skies around sunset time. These are mostly extracted from the berries rather than the cane (dried blackberries are ideal). However, the addition of canes and leaves, mainly of cultivated thornless varieties rather than wild ones, will strengthen the grey undertones of these shades.

There is a whole magical array of purples you can elicit from the fruit, which made me forget purple was my least favourite colour before I started dyeing with the stuff. I particularly love the moody lilac of the shirt dress (p166). To achieve it, I used a mix of dried berries (I foraged the shrivelled fruits that had turned black and crumbled like ash when I touched them), which I added to the cooking water from the maqluba recipe (p158), alongside a touch (about 4 tbsp) of iron-infused water. Playing with the quantities of this "recipe", with the occasional addition of chopped canes and leaves or even some used tea bags, I managed to extract all sorts of profoundly touching purples, from dampened lavender to greyish violets.

Using an iron mordant with the berries will produce spellbindingly deep, dusky blues, while adding an iron mordant to the pesky bramble branches and shoots will extract bluish-green, dusty greens.

As with any other natural dye, I cannot tell you the exact quantities I used to achieve each shade, as each colour had the unique depth afforded to it by the condition of the plant, the complexion of the tap water, and the base fabric. What I can promise you is that blackberry is sensitive to these changes like no other natural dyestuff, and that playing around to explore the possibilities of its rich pigments is one of the most satisfying natural dye experiences you are likely to have.

See pages 18–23 for more detailed information on dyestuff, mordants, and dye vat ratios.

Blackberry colour range

The Blackberry Shirt typically weighs 250g–300g (9–10oz), while the full-length shirt(dress) is in the area of 370g (12¾ oz). These tentative dye "recipes" are for 100g (3½ oz) of fabric – multiply the quantities as required and use enough water to cover the fabric. Bear in mind that the shade may vary depending on your fabric, water pH level, time in the foraging season, the freshness of the berries, and serendipity.

Moody lilac

Medium-weight French linen, mordanted with alum. Dyed with blackberry cooking water, strengthened with 50g (1¾oz) dried blackberries, 40g (1½oz) blackberry canes, and 1 tsp of iron-infused water for every 100g (3½oz) of fabric. Boiled and simmered for 2 hours, steeped overnight.

Purply pink

Medium-weight coarse linen, mordanted with alum. Dyed in an aluminum vat with blackberry cooking water, strengthened with 80g (2¾oz) fermented blackberries for every 100g (3½oz) of fabric. Boiled and simmered for 3 hours, steeped overnight.

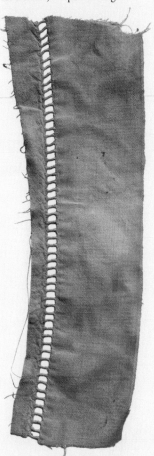

Faded rose

Medium-weight antique linen mordanted with alum. Dyed with blackberry cooking water, strengthened with 20g (¾oz) fermented blackberries and 1 used tea bag for every 100g (3½oz) of fabric. Boiled and simmered for 3 hours, steeped overnight.

Muddy magenta

Lightweight linen mordanted with alum. Dyed with blackberry cooking water, strengthened with 75g (2½oz) dried and fermented blackberries, 70g (2¼ oz) blackberry canes and leaves, and 1 tsp of copper-infused water for every 100g (3½oz) of fabric. Boiled and simmered for 2 hours, steeped overnight.

Dye *Blackberry*

Dusky blue

Medium-weight coarse antique linen. Dyed with blackberry cooking water, strengthened with 80g (2¾oz) dried and fermented blackberries, 1 tsp of iron-infused water, and 1 tbsp of iron sulphate for every 100g (3½oz) of fabric. Boiled and simmered for 2 hours, steeped for 4 hours.

Steel grey

Lightweight cheesecloth, dyed with blackberry cooking water, strengthened with 125g (4½oz) dried blackberries, 50g (1¾oz) blackberry canes and leaves, and 1 tbsp of iron sulphate for every 100g (3½oz) of fabric. Boiled and simmered for 2 hours, steeped for 5 hours.

Purplish blue

Medium-weight French linen. Dyed in an aluminum vat with blackberry cooking water, strengthened with 100g (3½oz) dried and fermented blackberries, 1 tsp of iron-infused water and 1 tbsp of iron sulphate for every 100g (3½oz) of fabric. Boiled and simmered for 2 hours, steeped for 5 hours.

The Blackberry Shirt(dress)

The Blackberry Shirt(dress) is a gender-neutral pattern, which you can cut in standard hip length or extend to the middle of the knee with a curved hem option. The longer version also includes a drawstring detail, which allows you to cinch in the waist for a more defined dress-like silhouette in this otherwise relaxed garment. It's the kind of thing you could wear and feel chic in an understated way. A fair warning: as sewing goes, this is the most difficult garment in the book. You will get there – like any other acquired skill, it's just a matter of time and practice.

Construction

Shown on the right are the pattern pieces for the Blackberry Shirt(dress) (please see Pattern Sheets 3 and 4).

Additionally to the fabric and interfacing, you'll also require 8 (shirt length) – 10 (dress length) buttons (at least 1cm/⅜in diameter) – 6–8 for the centre front and 2 for the back cuffs.

All seam allowances are 1cm (⅜in) unless otherwise stated.

Measurements

This garment is based on a relaxed fit menswear shirt with a wide neck opening feature. The measurements to consider here are bust, waist, and hips.

Please refer to the appendix on p221 for size charts and fabric requirements.

Please refer to the appendix for more details (p221).

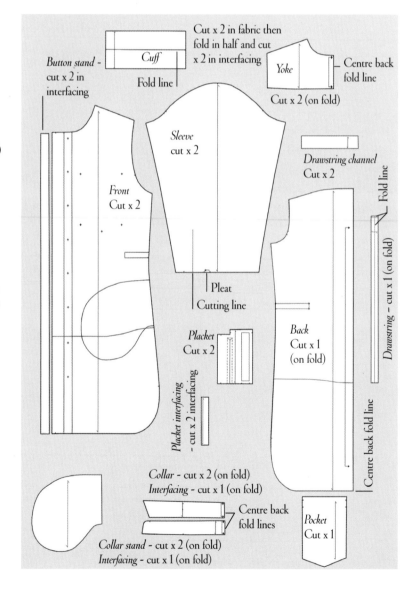

Button stand - cut x 2 in interfacing

Cuff
Cut x 2 in fabric then fold in half and cut x 2 in interfacing
Fold line

Yoke
Centre back fold line
Cut x 2 (on fold)

Sleeve
cut x 2

Drawstring channel
Cut x 2
Fold line

Front
Cut x 2

Drawstring – cut x 1 (on fold)

Pleat
Cutting line

Placket
Cut x 2

Back
Cut x 1
(on fold)

Placket interfacing - cut x 2 interfacing

Centre back fold line

Collar - cut x 2 (on fold)
Interfacing - cut x 1 (on fold)

Centre back fold lines

Pocket
Cut x 1

Collar stand - cut x 2 (on fold)
Interfacing - cut x 1 (on fold)

Method

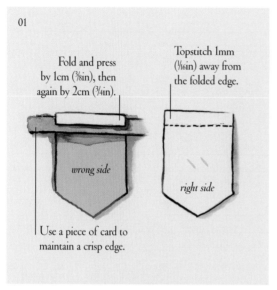

01

Fold and press
by 1cm (⅜in), then
again by 2cm (¾in).

Topstitch 1mm
(¹⁄₁₆in) away from
the folded edge.

wrong side

right side

Use a piece of card to
maintain a crisp edge.

02

a

wrong side

Fold and press
the rest of the
pocket seam
allowances by
1cm (⅜in).

Start with the
side edges and
finish with the
bottom edges.

b

All pocket seam
allowances pressed
and folded.

wrong side

01 Prepare the patch pocket

Fold and press the top edge of the pocket to the wrong side by 1cm (⅜in). Fold and press this edge over again by 2cm (¾in). Topstitch 1mm (¹⁄₁₆in) away from the folded edge, using the inside edge of your machine foot as a guide.

02 Fold and press the rest of the patch pocket seam allowances to the wrong side by 1cm (⅜in), starting with the side edges and finishing with the bottom edges (a) (b).

Before you begin

Tackling cuffs, a placket, and a shirt collar (alongside the less conventional curved hem) requires experience. If you're still building your confidence and skill set, the Onion Dress (p54) or Cabbage Shorts (p208) are the best projects to start with. Alternatively, a simpler variation of the shirt can be created by shortening the sleeves – allowing you to skip over the notorious placket (steps 11–15). I shorten mine by around 27cm (10½in) for a just-above-elbow length.

05

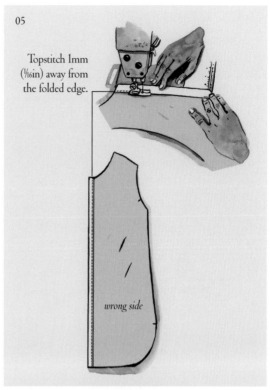

Topstitch 1mm (⅟₁₆in) away from the folded edge.

wrong side

03

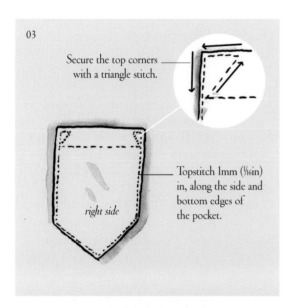

Secure the top corners with a triangle stitch.

Topstitch 1mm (⅟₁₆in) in, along the side and bottom edges of the pocket.

right side

04

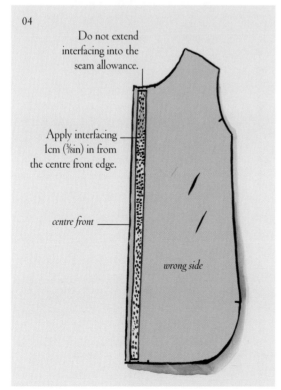

Do not extend interfacing into the seam allowance.

Apply interfacing 1cm (⅜in) in from the centre front edge.

centre front

wrong side

03 **Sew the pocket to the front**

Pin the pocket in place on the front, according to the markings on the pattern. Topstitch along the side and bottom edges, 1mm (⅟₁₆in) from the edge. For longevity, secure the top corners with a triangle stitch (see step 3 of the Nettle Duster, p91).

04 **Sew the button stands:**

Apply interfacing to the wrong side of the shirt front, 1cm (⅜in) in from the centre front edge. To reduce bulk in the neck and hemline, the interfacing should not extend into the seam allowance. Take time to measure and place it accurately. Repeat for the other shirt front.

05 Fold and press the centre front edge over to the wrong side of the fabric by 1cm (⅜in), then fold and press this edge again by 2.5cm (1in). Topstitch 1mm (⅟₁₆in) along the folded edge, using the inside edge of your machine foot as a guide. Press. Repeat for the other front piece.

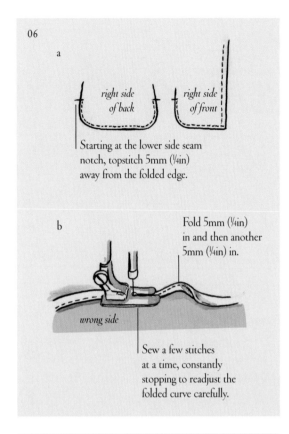

06

a

right side of back   *right side of front*

Starting at the lower side seam notch, topstitch 5mm (¼in) away from the folded edge.

b

Fold 5mm (¼in) in and then another 5mm (¼in) in.

wrong side

Sew a few stitches at a time, constantly stopping to readjust the folded curve carefully.

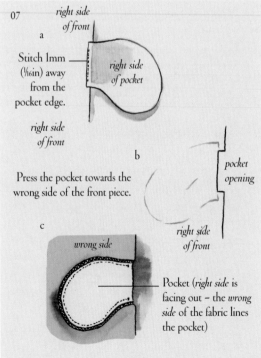

07

a

right side of front

Stitch 1mm (¹⁄₁₆in) away from the pocket edge.

right side of pocket

right side of front

Press the pocket towards the wrong side of the front piece.

b

pocket opening

right side of front

c

wrong side

Pocket (*right side* is facing out – the *wrong side* of the fabric lines the pocket)

If you are making the shirt variation, skip to step 8 (you will complete the hem in step 32).

06 Stitch the curved hem (dress only)

Starting at the lower side seam notch on one of the front pieces, topstitch 5mm (¼in) in from the edge on the right side of the fabric, until you reach the centre front. This will serve as a guide for sewing the curved hem. Repeat for the other front piece. Repeat for the back piece, starting and ending at the lower side seam notches (a).

Fold and press the hemline to the wrong side of the fabric by 5mm (¼in) and then by another 5mm (¼in). I find it's futile to try and use pins when sewing this curved hem. It is best to sew a few stitches at a time, constantly stopping to readjust the folded curve carefully (b). You may also find it helpful to snip 3–4mm (around ⅛in) notches into the curve, which will help alleviate the tension as you fold the hem. Repeat for the other front piece and the back. Press well with plenty of steam to flatten completely.

07 Sew the pockets (dress only):

Following the pocket bag notches, pin one of the pocket bag pieces to the front piece, right sides together. Stitch along the straight edge, 1cm (⅜in) from the edge. Fold the pocket bag over along the stitching line, so that both the pocket bag and the front right are right side up. Stitch 1mm (¹⁄₁₆in) in from the pocket edge (a). This will keep the seam allowance tucked neatly to one side and strengthen the pocket opening.

Cut 1cm (⅜in) notches into the front body side seam, taking care not to snip through the pocket stitches. Press the pocket to the wrong side of the front to create a neat pocket opening line (b).

08

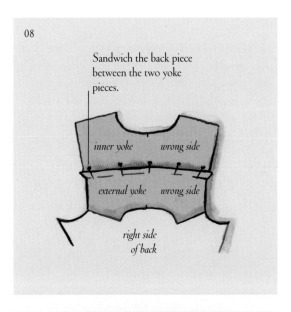

Sandwich the back piece between the two yoke pieces.

inner yoke   *wrong side*

external yoke   *wrong side*

right side of back

09

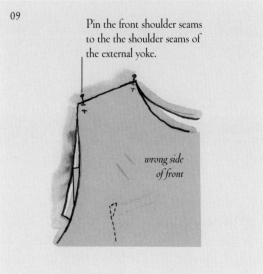

Pin the front shoulder seams to the the shoulder seams of the external yoke.

wrong side of front

Pin a second pocket bag on top of the first, wrong sides together, aligning the curved edges. Note that this piece is 1cm (⅜in) longer on the side-seam edge. Stitch around the curved edges, then finish with an overlock or zigzag stitch (c). Press. Repeat step 7 for the other pocket.

08 **Sew the yoke**

Pin the yoke pieces to the back, aligning the bottom edge of the yokes with the top edge of the back and sandwiching the back piece in between. (The external yoke and the back will be right sides together; the right side of the inner yoke will be against the wrong side of the back.) Stitch all three layers together. Press the seam allowances together, then flip the yoke pieces up and press the seam flat.

09 Pin the front shoulder seam to the shoulder seam of the external yoke, right sides together. Keep the inner yoke separate. Stitch along the shoulder seam. Press. Repeat for the other shoulder.

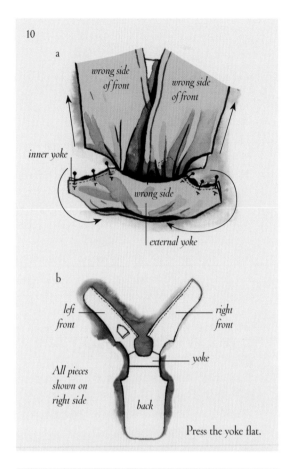

10 **a**

wrong side
of front

wrong side
of front

inner yoke

wrong side

external yoke

b

left
front

right
front

yoke

All pieces
shown on
right side

back

Press the yoke flat.

10 Pin the right side of the inner yoke to the right side of the joined shoulder seam. Sew along the existing stitch line. Bag out – pull inside out through the neckhole – and press the shoulder seam flat (a). Press the yoke flat (b). Repeat for the other shoulder.

11 **Sew the placket**

Mark the cutting line on the wrong side of the sleeve. Next, mark the cutting line and its 7mm (¼in) "frame" on the wrong side of the placket piece, as they appear on the pattern. Apply the interfacing to the wrong side of the placket, according to the markings on the pattern. Press the long side edges of the placket as well as the external placket top edge to the wrong side by 1cm (⅜in) in (a). Next, fold the long edges in again to meet the marked frame edges and press (b). (You may find it useful to use a piece of card to maintain a crisp edge.) Then unfold.

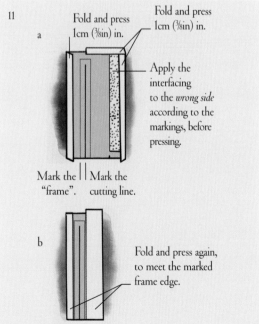

11 **a**

Fold and press
1cm (⅜in) in.

Fold and press
1cm (⅜in) in.

Apply the
interfacing
to the *wrong side*
according to the
markings, before
pressing.

Mark the   Mark the
"frame".   cutting line.

b

Fold and press again,
to meet the marked
frame edge.

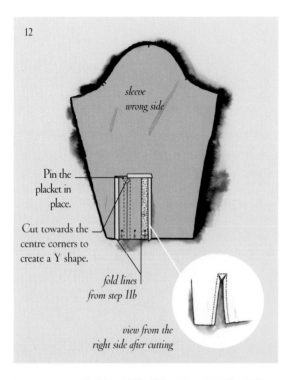

12

*sleeve
wrong side*

Pin the
placket in
place.

Cut towards the
centre corners to
create a Y shape.

*fold lines
from step 11b*

*view from the
right side after cutting*

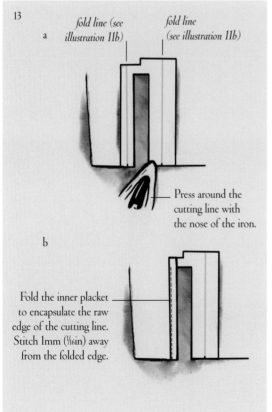

13

a

*fold line (see
illustration 11b)*

*fold line
(see illustration 11b)*

Press around the
cutting line with
the nose of the iron.

b

Fold the inner placket
to encapsulate the raw
edge of the cutting line.
Stitch 1mm (¹⁄₁₆in) away
from the folded edge.

12   Pin the placket to the sleeve, so the wrong side of the
sleeve and the wrong side of the placket are facing out.
Make sure the cutting lines of the sleeve and placket align.
Stitch the 7mm (¼in) "frame" around the cutting line. Cut
carefully through the cutting line of both the sleeve and the
placket pieces to create the placket opening. When you get
to 1cm (⅜in) below the top of the frame, snip diagonally
towards the corners to create a Y shape – get as close as
you can to the stitch line, but be careful not to cut into it!

13   Turn the sleeve so the right side is facing up, then
turn the placket to the right side of the sleeve, pulling
it through the cut edge. Press around the rectangular
opening (a). Fold the inner placket (the narrower side)
along the fold line pressed in step 11, then fold it over
the cutting line so that it encloses the raw edge. Stitch
1mm (¹⁄₁₆in) away from the folded edge to secure the
inner placket in place and press (b). Sew with the
right side of the sleeve facing up to align both fold
lines as you sew, to ensure that you catch both sides
in the stitching.

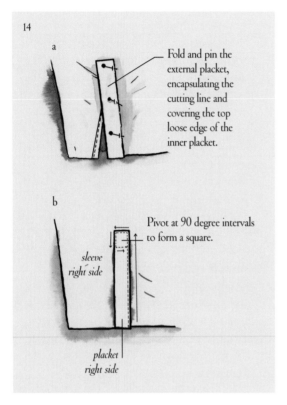

a

Fold and pin the external placket, encapsulating the cutting line and covering the top loose edge of the inner placket.

b

Pivot at 90 degree intervals to form a square.

*sleeve
right side*

*placket
right side*

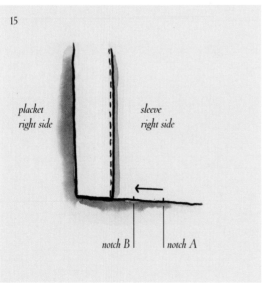

*placket
right side*

*sleeve
right side*

notch B *notch A*

14 Fold the external placket (the wider side) along the fold line pressed in step 11 (see illustration 11b), then fold it over the raw edge of the cutting line, so that it encloses it and also covers the top loose edge of the inner placket (the narrower side). Pin in place (a). Starting from the bottom, stitch 1mm (1/16in) in from the edge. When you reach the top right corner, pivot 90 degrees, keeping the machine needle in the fabric. Pivot again once you reach the left corner and sew 2cm (3/4in) down, pivoting again to form a square (b). Take it slowly and carefully, one stitch at a time, as this is a fragile area.

15 **Sew the bottom sleeve pleat**
Pin notch A on top of notch B. Stitch 7mm (1/4in) in from the edge. Press. Repeat steps 11–15 for the other sleeve.

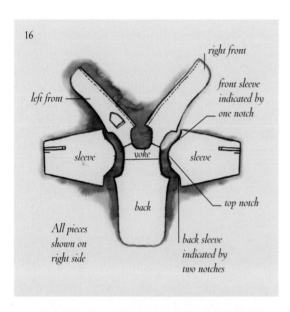

16

right front

left front

front sleeve
indicated by
one notch

sleeve   yoke   sleeve

back

top notch

All pieces
shown on
right side

back sleeve
indicated by
two notches

16 Sew the sleeve head

The front of the sleeve is indicated by one notch and the back by two notches. Pin these to the corresponding notches in the armhole, with right sides together. Pin the top sleeve notch to the shoulder seam. As this is a relaxed, menswear-inspired cut, there is no ease in the sleeve head. Stitch in place and finish with an overlock or zigzag stitch. Press the seam allowance towards the sleeve. Repeat for the other sleeve.

17 Sew the sleeve and body side seam

Fold the garment right sides together and pin together the sleeve and body side seams. Sew each side in one continuous seam: start from the bottom of the sleeve and work up the sleeve, through the armhole, and down the side seam, ending at the hemline. Finish with an overlock or zigzag stitch. Press the seam allowance towards the back.

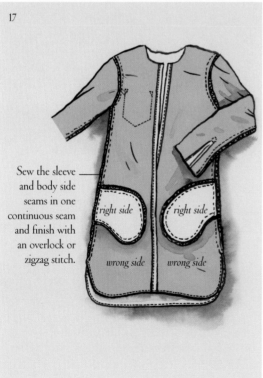

17

Sew the sleeve
and body side
seams in one
continuous seam
and finish with
an overlock or
zigzag stitch.

right side   right side

wrong side   wrong side

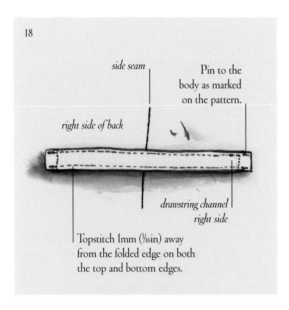

18

side seam

Pin to the body as marked on the pattern.

right side of back

drawstring channel right side

Topstitch 1mm (¹⁄₁₆in) away from the folded edge on both the top and bottom edges.

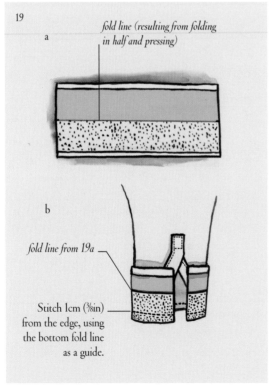

19

a

fold line (resulting from folding in half and pressing)

b

fold line from 19a

Stitch 1cm (³⁄₈in) from the edge, using the bottom fold line as a guide.

If you are making the shirt variation, progress to step 19.

18 **Sew the drawstring channels (dress only):**
Press the short edges of one of the drawstring channels to the wrong side by 5mm (¼in) and then by another 5mm (¼in) and topstitch. Press the long edges to the wrong side by 1cm (³⁄₈in) in and pin to the dress as marked on the pattern, right side out. Topstitch 1mm (¹⁄₁₆in) away from the fold on both the top and bottom edges. Repeat for the other drawstring channel.

19 **Sew the cuffs**
Apply interfacing to the wrong side of half of the cuff. Press the seam allowance on both long sides to the wrong side by 1cm (³⁄₈in), then fold the cuff in half, right side out, and press again (a).

Pin the cuff to the end of the sleeve, right sides together and aligning the interfaced half with the sleeve's raw edges. Note that the cuff extends past the placket by 1cm (³⁄₈in) on each side. Stitch in place, using the pressed fold line as a guide.

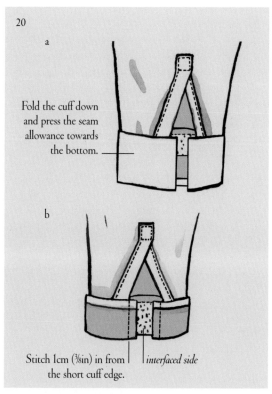

20

a

Fold the cuff down and press the seam allowance towards the bottom. —

b

Stitch 1cm (⅜in) in from the short cuff edge. | interfaced side

21

Topstitch 1mm (¹⁄₁₆in) away from the edge. —

Make sure the stitching aligns on both sides.

20 Fold the cuff down and press the seam allowance towards the bottom of the cuff – the right sides of both cuff and sleeve will be facing out (a). Fold the cuff in half along the centre press line, so that the right sides of the cuff fabric are facing together and the folded edge of the non-interfaced side is facing out – you will be able to see the interfaced side through the placket opening. Pin and stitch the short cuff edges (b).

21 Bag out the cuff, so the wrong sides of the fabric are facing together, and the right sides are facing out. Using the edge of your scissors, carefully push out the corners. Press well. Pin the outer cuff to the right side of the sleeve. Pin with care, making sure it overlaps perfectly with the inner cuff line. Topstitch slowly and carefully 1mm (¹⁄₁₆in) away from the edge. (Make sure the stitching aligns as you go along – falling 1mm (¹⁄₁₆in) away from the edge on both sides of the cuff.) Press well. Repeat steps 19–21 for the other cuff.

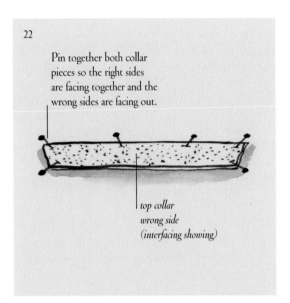

22

Pin together both collar
pieces so the right sides
are facing together and the
wrong sides are facing out.

top collar
wrong side
(interfacing showing)

22 Sew the collar

The collar is cut in two pieces – the top collar, which
will be facing out and visible when the shirt(dress) is
worn, and the under collar, which will be in view if you
choose to pull the collar up.

Apply interfacing to the wrong side of the top collar.
Next, pin the top and under collars right sides together.

23 Stitch together around three sides, 7mm (¼in) from the
edge. When you are one stitch away from the first
pivot point, use the hack on p137 to achieve a sharp
corner (a–d). Repeat for the other corner.

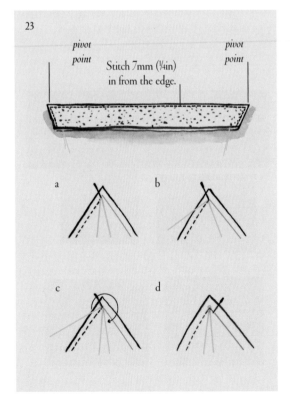

23

*pivot
point*

*pivot
point*

Stitch 7mm (¼in)
in from the edge.

a   b

c   d

24

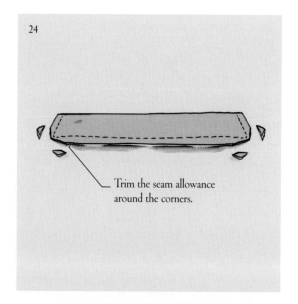

Trim the seam allowance
around the corners.

26

Apply interfacing to
the wrong side of the
outer collar stand piece.

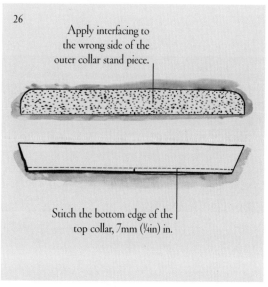

Stitch the bottom edge of the
top collar, 7mm (¼in) in.

25

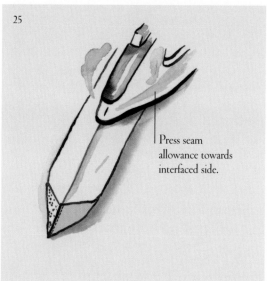

Press seam
allowance towards
interfaced side.

24 Trim the seam allowance around the corners to
reduce bulk.

25 Press the top, long, seam flat, with the seam allowance
pushed towards the interfaced side. Take it slowly –
a nice crisp collar is a mark of a finely made shirt.

Turn the collar right side out, using a pencil or the
blade of your scissors to push out the corner. (Be
gentle! The corner is particularly fragile once you have
trimmed the seam allowance.) Pull the thread inserts to
perfect the corners, then cut and discard. Press all over
with plenty of steam.

26 Apply interfacing to the wrong side of the inner collar
stand. Press the bottom edge of the non-interfaced
collar stand to the wrong side by 7mm (¼in). Stitch
the bottom edge of the top collar 7mm (¼in) from
the edge.

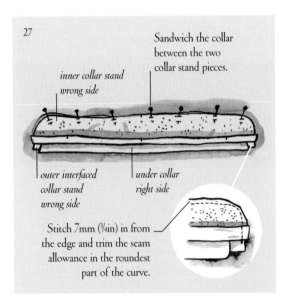

27

Sandwich the collar between the two collar stand pieces.

inner collar stand
wrong side

outer interfaced
collar stand
wrong side

under collar
right side

Stitch 7mm (¼in) in from
the edge and trim the seam
allowance in the roundest
part of the curve.

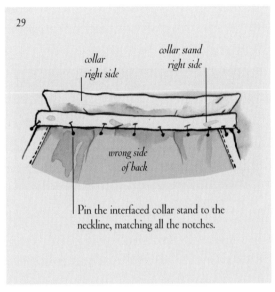

29

collar
right side

collar stand
right side

wrong side
of back

Pin the interfaced collar stand to the
neckline, matching all the notches.

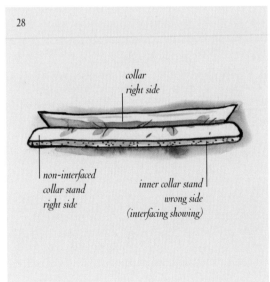

28

collar
right side

non-interfaced
collar stand
right side

inner collar stand
wrong side
(interfacing showing)

27 Matching the centre back notches, sandwich the collar between the two collar stand pieces, with the right sides of both collar stands facing inwards; the interfaced collar stand should be against the top collar. Stitch around the curved section 7mm (¼in) from the edge, leaving the long straight edge open. Trim the seam allowance around the roundest part of the curve.

28 Pull the collar stand down and press well.

29 Attach the collar to the shirt(dress)

Pin the interfaced collar stand to the neckline, with the right side of the collar stand against the wrong side of the garment, matching all the notches. Stitch together using a 7mm (¼in) seam allowance. Press. Carefully pin the remaining collar stand piece to the neckline. The pre-pressed seam allowance indicates where your stitch will be. Try to overlap it as close as possible to the seam created in the previous stage. Stitch 1mm (¹⁄₁₆in) away from the edge, using the inside edge of your machine foot as a guide. Stop every few stitches to check that the bottom seam is even all the way round, as the stitch line will be visible on both sides. Press the collar and the entire garment.

30

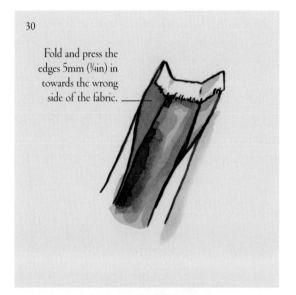

Fold and press the edges 5mm (¼in) in towards the wrong side of the fabric.

32

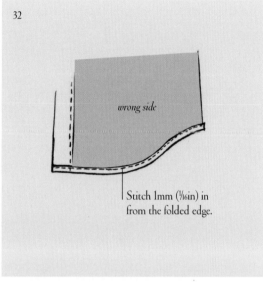

wrong side

Stitch 1mm (⅟₁₆in) in from the folded edge.

31

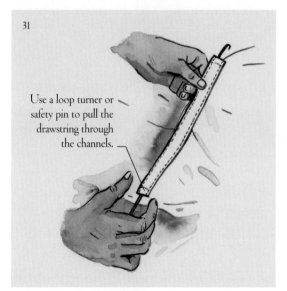

Use a loop turner or safety pin to pull the drawstring through the channels.

30 **Sew the drawstring (dress only)**
Fold and press the first one short edge and then both long edges to the wrong side by 5mm (¼in). Fold and press the drawstring in half, so the right sides are facing out. Topstitch all around, 1mm (⅟₁₆in) away from the edge.

31 Attach a safety pin or a loop turner to the end of the drawstring and use it to pull the drawstring through the drawstring channels.

32 **Sew the hem (shirt only)**
Fold and press the hem to the wrong side by 5mm (¼in), then again by another 5mm (¼in), and stitch 1mm (⅟₁₆in) in from the folded edge. Press well, using plenty of steam to flatten the hem completely.

33

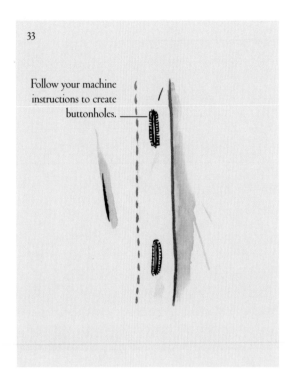

Follow your machine
instructions to create
buttonholes.

33 Sew the buttonholes and buttons:

Now that the garment is ready, try it on to check if the
buttonhole markings suit your figure. Like many other
finishing details, the positioning of fastening accessories
can make a big difference for different body shapes.
While patterns are not as straightforward to alter,
changing button positions is easy – play around using
pins in front of the mirror to find the positioning that
suits you best. Once you make your markings (or
decide to stick to the ones marked on the pattern),
follow your machine instructions to create buttonholes.
Sew on buttons to correspond with the buttonholes.
Alternatively, sew on snap fastenings.

Cabbage

For me, the greatest joy of growing cabbage is not in the final produce, nor even in the harvesting process. No, my favourite part is looking at cabbage plants – undoubtedly one of the most magnificent organisms in the vegetable kingdom. It is an excellent example of how much we miss if we only know cabbage as we purchase it. We lose out on its gargantuan flower-like structure, made out of meaty, vein-covered leaves, its beautiful colour determined by the soil's pH level. It is just as well as cabbage, like many plants grown as annuals in the brassica family, requires some care. It's not the kind of "sow and see how it goes" crop – it isn't foolproof. What it will reward you with, other than its stunning appearance, is almost year-round growth. It will provide you with a delicious and nutritious harvest in a time when there is little else around. There are many wonderful cabbage varieties and an actual multi-seasonal harvest will rely on a timely sown ensemble. In this chapter, the spotlight will be on the red cabbage, as it provides the most dazzling array of colour: all the blues and purples of the ocean and sky – the kind of eternal palette that you'd expect from such a captivating plant.

Sow Cabbage

Many plants are challenging to sow from seed, their germination process long and erratic. You find yourself moving their propagated pots from one windowsill to another throughout the short days, trying to capture every ray of winter sunshine. This is not the case with cabbages, which are surprisingly easy to grow from seed, given that they are otherwise a rather attention-demanding crop. Every year, I find myself in awe of these nimble seedlings, which seem as eager as I am for the arrival of spring, and with it the official start of the growing season.

My first sowing would usually be in the bleakest part of winter, the last week of February. These are my summer and autumn cabbages, named, somewhat confusingly, after their harvesting season. Spring cabbages accordingly are harvested after maturing slowly through winter, and are sown in late summer. I sow both summer and autumn cabbages in the same session as other brassicas: white cabbage, kale, broccoli, and one of my all-time favourites – kohlrabi. As these relatives require similar (and rather specific) growing conditions, they happily cohabit side by side.

Growing from seed

I start my cabbages indoors, as I do with anything that I sow on some of the coldest days of the year, or that are particularly favoured by slugs. I sometimes use seed trays or modules (a good-quality one can serve you for years), but I increasingly prefer to use my own makeshift seedling pots that give them a bit more room to grow. These can be made out of any so-called disposable container that can be reused before it is recycled: cut back oat milk cartons, the odd paper takeaway cup, soya yoghurt pots (their transparent lids make for an excellent seedling "greenhouse"). Anything

that I can furnish drainage holes in with the little drill I use when marking darts and pocket placements as I cut sewing patterns. I fill them with good-quality, peat-free seedling compost, giving it a good soak before even taking the seeds out of the packet.

When you sow cabbages, the most important thing to consider is how many you could actually fit in your garden. It is all too easy to forget that the tiny seeds develop into extraordinary plants that can grow incredibly tall and wide, requiring a lot of space and

immense amounts of energy to produce just a single cabbage head. As seeds, however, they are tricky to handle. I'm always struck by their resemblance to brown mustard seeds, one of these spices you can easily add too much of due to the small size and bouncy nature of its perfectly round balls.

I pour a few onto a plate and then place them individually 1cm (½in) deep at the centre of each pot, and cover lightly with a sprinkle of compost. I keep them in a heated propagator and make sure they stay moist by spraying them with water until they germinate – usually about four days, but no longer than a week. I then move them to a sunny windowsill as, from this point, their development is light-dependent. Much as in feng shui, six is the lucky number here: seedlings are mature enough to transplant roughly six weeks after sowing, when they reach at least 6cm (2½in) in height and grow six leaves. At that point I start hardening them up, putting them outside for an increasing number of hours every day, allowing them to slowly acclimatize to the distinctly different conditions from the coziness of indoors.

Varieties

"Red drumhead" The most popular, and therefore most commonly available, variety. It is characterized by its fine texture and solid, dark round head. Sown early in the year, it is ready to harvest by early autumn.

"Rovite" This is a reliable, hardy autumn or spring variety, depending on when you plant it. It performs well in unremarkable soils and dry conditions.

"Kalibos" and **"Red flame"** Both are crossbreeds of the white pointed cabbage and red cabbage – the former is an autumn variety, while the latter is a hardy spring cropper.

Cultivate *Cabbage*

Cabbage thrives in full sunlight and when grown in fertile yet firm, free-draining soil. Dig in rotted manure as a fertilizer at least once a month and preferably one season ahead, to let the ground settle undisturbed. Tread over the soil to compact it even further, and then rake to even the surface before you plant. Cabbages are susceptible to changes in pH levels, and this sensitivity starts in the soil. The ideal level of pH is 6–7.5, but they can handle a slight divergence either way.

Make sure you allocate enough space – 45cm (18in) – between each cabbage and row. To ensure robust and steady plants, you need to get the seedlings deep into the ground, deeper than may seem reasonable. Depending on growing conditions they will hopefully be about 12–15cm (5–6in). Dig a big hole, at least 10cm (4in) deep, so that only the leaves and top stems are above earth level when placed in. Puddle the seedlings in: fill the hole with water several times before covering them with soil and firming around the plant. It will give the cabbages a good head start, but make sure you keep them moist throughout the season, and particularly during the core growth period when they develop most of their foliage and build a strong root system. This, alongside a nitrogen feed every 3–4 weeks and regular weeding, will encourage them to form a solid layer of compact leaves in the edible middle part, interestingly referred to as both the cabbage's head and heart.

Cabbage fly prevention

More than any other plant featured in this book, cabbage attracts a large number of pests. The most common is the white cabbage butterfly, which love to lay their eggs on the plants' leaves. The caterpillars that emerge can devour your plant at a staggering speed.

The best way to prevent this is by covering it with a fine, mesh-like net, which also prevents pigeons from picking at the much-loved young brassicas. I still get the odd fly wandering in, as no net is hermetic in the face of changing weather conditions. If an infestation of white cabbage butterfly starts, the most efficient management tactic is to remove the caterpillars by hand, alongside the dark green, caviar-like eggs that they lay at the bottom of the leaves. It is a bit tedious as it's time-consuming but, once I get used to it, I find it soothing, forensically examining each of these gorgeous patterned leaves.

....

Potted cabbage?

Space issues can make cabbages an unpopular container crop, but you could grow them in large pots or tubs (not bags), as long as you are happy to dedicate one to each plant. This will yield smaller cabbage heads than the ones you grow in the soil or your average store-bought cabbages. Nevertheless, they look quite stunning on roof terraces or balconies, partially because of the sheer surprise of finding cabbages in such places. They are also less likely to be affected by pests and disease in these environments.

....

Soil-borne risks

I feel nothing but stoicism for snails and slugs, which became an acute problem with the recent heavy summer downpours. They love nutritious cabbage leaves, and you can often find many of them picking at the back of the lower ones. Organic slug control is possible, and something you will have to master for many other crops. I find that beer traps are handy around the cabbage bed. Another helpful tip for both pests is placing easy-to-grow decoy plants between rows. The cabbage fly favours nasturtiums, while the slugs would enjoy basil leaves or any salad leaf.

Like many things in life, prevention is wiser than curing or managing when it comes to cabbage root fly. You can do so easily by creating "cabbage collars" – 10-15cm (4-6in) diameter discs cut from cardboard. These will protect the flies' preferred egg-laying place by the base of the stem. Rotating your brassica's growing bed seasonally will also help protect them from soil-borne diseases, but won't eliminate the threat completely. The worst is clubroot, a fungus that makes the roots swell and deform grotesquely. It is more likely to live in acidic soil so, if lime treatment hasn't helped, consider growing your plant in a raised bed, with the plants spaced even further apart, promoting drainage, which may prevent a build-up of acidity in the soil.

Harvest *Cabbage*

Theoretically speaking, cabbages are ready to harvest at any given time once their heads have formed. Indeed, sometimes when a pest situation gets out of control, I pick them young. But if I can, I try to keep summer and autumn cabbages going until the very end of their growing season to enjoy that special moment when you pick a genuine prized vegetable. Cabbages don't come any better than ones that are large and that you have been cultivating for an awfully long time.

Spring's cabbages are naturally smaller than their autumn and summer counterparts and I aim to pick them before the summer heat sets in. Cabbages are at their prime harvesting time when they resist a light press at the centre of their head. If there is a bit of give, wait a little longer to enjoy them at their most dense and crispy. When consumed fresh, they will taste nothing like any shop-bought cabbage.

The right harvest moment can be fleeting, though. If heavy rain is forecast at the end of the summer and beginning of autumn, pick heads that are big

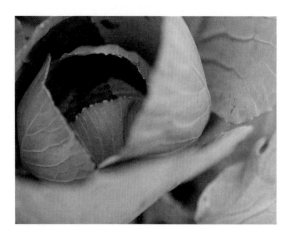

enough before the rain hits, as it may cause them to split and risk water damage running through the precious leaves.

To harvest, grab the stalk a few leaves below the cabbage head and cut with a sharp knife. These surrounding leaves are also edible, although most people find them too hard and fibrous, even after cooking. In this case, they could come to good use in the dye vat.

I read that if you cut the stalk cleanly and then form a 1cm-deep (½in) cross in the middle, you can encourage a second small head on the same plant. I wouldn't quite classify it as a gardening myth, but I have never managed it. What's more, even Mr Sadiq has never achieved this second coming. Like most things, I'd encourage you to give it a go, but don't be disheartened if you don't accomplish this extraordinary feat. Instead, plan a good succession of cabbages, whether red, white, or a crinkly Savoy, which will reward you with a good yield all year round.

Cabbage Oysters

Serves 4

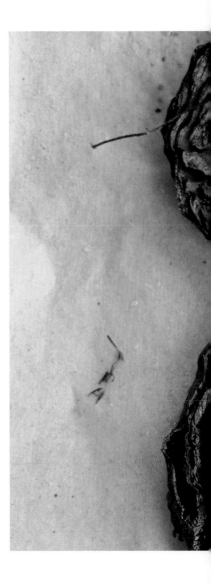

Although I have never tasted them, I feel confident that cabbage oysters taste nothing like real oysters. Still, I had the audacity to name this dish after the sea delicacy, as it shares its mesmerizing appearance – an elusive construct of layers within layers, the kind of food that you eat with your eyes. While they taste nothing like the sea, the Earl Grey does infuse these elaborate cabbage steaks with a subtle bergamot aroma, boosting their romantic attributes. Their tenderness transcends into the dye vat: the colour produced by dyeing with the strained cooking water is a stunningly low-saturated mix of purple, brown, and burgundy – a shade that looks "aged" to start with.

Ingredients

For the stock
1 onion, cut into quarters
4 garlic cloves, crushed
1 leek, cut into chunks
3 carrots, cut into chunks
1 small celeriac, cut into chunks
3 celery stalks, cut into chunks
½ green chilli
4 bay leaves
1 tbsp sea salt flakes
1 tsp black peppercorns

1 tsp allspice berries (optional)
1 tsp chopped ginger
2 Earl Grey tea bags

1 red cabbage
4 tbsp olive oil
1 tsp sea salt
freshly ground black pepper
a few sprigs of thyme
a squeeze of lime juice (optional)

Method

01 In a large saucepan, cover the stock ingredients with
    2 litres/3½ pints/8½ cups of water. Bring to the boil,
    then reduce to a simmer and cook for 2 hours. Pass
    through a sieve and return to the saucepan.

02 Cut the cabbage down the middle, splitting it into two
    halves. Hold each half on its side with the flat part either on
    the left or right, and cut again down the middle. Keep any
    discarded leaves, such as damaged outer ones, for the dye.

03 Simmer the four cabbage pieces in the stock for 15
    minutes, then drain the liquid into a bowl and reserve
    for the dye.

04 Heat the oven to 180°C/160°C fan/350°F/Gas 4.
    Line a large baking tray with greaseproof paper. Lay
    the cabbage pieces on top, drizzle with oil, sprinkle
    with salt and pepper, and decorate with thyme sprigs.
    Roast for 25 minutes, or until just crispy at the edges
    and tender in the centre. Serve warm or at room
    temperature, with a squeeze of lime if you wish.

Cabbage Kugel

Serves 4

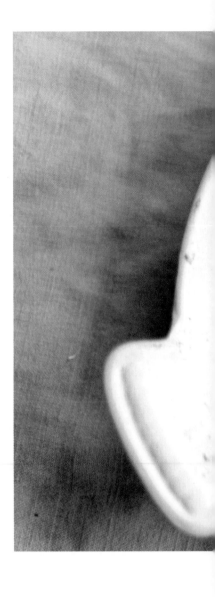

Kugel, the delightful sweet Jewish dairy casserole, is one of my all-time favourite puddings. I love it so much that once I managed to veganize it sufficiently, I started thinking of savoury versions so I wouldn't feel guilty for having it for dinner. This is one of my favourites. Above all else, kugel is a study of textures – a good one is a fine balance of creamy body and crunchy crust. I like to chop the cabbage the same width as the noodles I am using, so they interweave homogeneously once baked, adding a subtle chew to each bite. The walnuts enhance this tension as well as the sweet–savoury complexion of the cabbage. They make a lovely topping, too, their golden nuggets scattered over the cloudy, violet surface.

Ingredients

300g/10oz/4 cups red cabbage, chopped

100g/3½oz brown rice noodles

2 shallot onions, peeled and chopped (save the skins for dyeing)

2 garlic cloves, peeled and chopped

250g/9oz silken tofu

3 tbsp tahini

3 tbsp oat milk

juice of ½ lemon

½ tsp caraway seeds

½ tsp dried thyme

2 tbsp nutritional yeast

1½ tsp sea salt

freshly ground black pepper

90g/3oz/¾ cup walnuts, chopped, plus 30g/1oz/¼ cup to serve

Method

01 In separate bowls, soak the cabbage and noodles in freshly boiled water for 10 minutes. Drain and allow to cool. Save the cabbage water for the dye.

02 Heat the oven to 200°C/180°C fan/400°F/Gas 6. Grease a 23-cm/9-in baking dish with a depth of 5cm/2in. Add the soaked cabbage, noodles, and the rest of the ingredients. Mix to combine, using a spoon or your hands, and pour into the baking dish. Bake for 25–30 minutes or until the crust is golden.

03 Remove from the oven and let it cool for 10 minutes. Top with the remaining chopped walnuts and serve.

Stuffed Cabbage

Serves 4

You may not think of stuffed cabbage as a culinary phenomenon, but it is one of the most all-encompassing, border-breaking dishes I've ever encountered. It is common to the cuisines of eastern and western Europe, much of western Asia, northern China, and parts of north Africa. I found this out when I was trying to ascertain whether my version was closer to the Romanian or the Polish one. As it happens, it is a mixture of both, with touches of the Iraqi, German, and Hungarian dishes. My insistence on serving them on mamaliga, the Transylvanian version of polenta, makes this dish unquestionably Romanian. Although delicious on their own, serving them on top of the creamy porridge-y corn is peak comfort food – an almost pudding-like main.

Ingredients

For the stuffed cabbages
1 large red cabbage
1 red onion, peeled and chopped
  (save the skin for dyeing)
4 garlic cloves, peeled and chopped
1 courgette, chopped
1 tomato, grated
1 tsp baharat
½ tsp cinnamon
¼ tsp nutmeg
150g/5½oz/¾ cup brown
  basmati rice
2 tbsp tomato purée
1 tbsp date molasses
1½ tsp sea salt
freshly ground black pepper
60g/2¼oz/½ cup walnuts, chopped
20g/¾oz parsley leaves, chopped
20g/¾oz mint leaves, chopped

For the sauce
3 tbsp olive oil
1 red onion, peeled and chopped
  (save the skin for dyeing)
3 garlic cloves, peeled and chopped
½ can chopped tomatoes (200g/7oz)
12 cherry tomatoes, halved
1 tbsp sweet paprika
¼ tsp spicy paprika
1 tbsp date molasses

For the mamaliga
  (to serve – optional)
1 700ml/24fl oz/3 cups oat milk
35g/4¾oz/1 cup coarse cornmeal
1 tbsp vegan butter
1 tbsp nutritional yeast
1½ tsp sea salt
freshly ground black pepper

Method

01 Remove the cabbage core with a sharp knife (save it and any other discarded pieces for the dye) and soak in a bowl of freshly boiled water for 8 minutes – this will ease the leaf-peeling process . Meanwhile, bring a large saucepan of water to the boil. Peel 10–12 of the largest leaves and submerge them in the water. Cook for 8–12 minutes, until the leaves are pliable enough to roll. Remove and leave to cool (save the cooking water for dyeing). Chop the remaining uncooked leaves.

02 Heat the oil in a saucepan. Lower the heat, add the onion, and cook for 5–7 minutes, until translucent. Stir in the garlic and cook for another minute. Add the chopped cabbage, courgette, tomato, and spices, and cook for 2 minutes, stirring occasionally. Add the rice, stir to combine, then cover with freshly boiled water. Stir in the tomato purée, date molasses, salt, and pepper to taste, then simmer for 30 minutes. Remove, allow to cool, then stir in the walnuts and herbs.

03 Use the same saucepan to make the sauce. Heat the oil, add the onion, and cook for 5 minutes. Add the garlic and cook for another minute. Add the rest of the ingredients and simmer for 10 minutes.

04 While the sauce is simmering, assemble the cabbages. Place 2–3 tbsp of the filling towards the bottom end of each leaf and roll upwards until the filling is covered by cabbage. Then fold the left and right corners towards the centre and continue to roll until sealed.

05 Heat the oven to 180°C/160°C fan/350°F/Gas 4. Arrange the cabbages so they sit snugly at the bottom of a large cast-iron pan or roasting tin. Pour the sauce on top and bake covered for 30 minutes, then uncover and continue baking for another 20 minutes, or until the sauce has thickened and the top is slightly browned.

06 In the meantime, make the mamaliga. Heat the oat milk on a medium heat in a medium-sized pan. Just before it starts boiling, lower the heat to the lowest setting, and add the cornmeal in a slow stream, whisking continuously. Continue whisking until it thickens and pulls away from the sides. The time will vary according to the type of cornmeal. Stir in the remaining ingredients.

07 Serve the stuffed cabbages over the mamaliga hot or on their own. Like many stuffed vegetables, they can taste even better after a night in the fridge.

Cabbage Lasagne

Serves 6

The pasta is never the star of the classic lasagne (if there is such a thing). Even if you go through the traditional effort of making your own, the sheets merely serve as the foundation, or supporting blocks, for all the goodness encased between them – the comforting ragù, velvety béchamel sauce and herby tomatoes. This is the part where the divergence from a pasta-based lasagne becomes significant as the leaves hold a character of their own, adding a crispy, chewy texture, a subtle sweetness, beautiful colour, and intriguing patterns. Some prefer it because it is a gluten-free, lower carb option, but I like it for its sheer opulence. It makes a good vegan dish for Christmas lunch, which is the red cabbage's finest hour anyway.

Ingredients

2 red cabbages

For the lentil ragú
125g/4½ oz/½ cup Puy or brown lentils
2 tbsp olive oil
1 onion, chopped
2 garlic cloves, peeled and chopped
1 leek, chopped
200g/7oz chestnut mushrooms
1 tsp vegan Worcestershire sauce
1 tsp smoked paprika
1 tsp baharat
1 tbsp nutritional yeast
1 tsp sea salt

For the creamed greens tahini béchamel
2 tbsp olive oil
1 onion, chopped
2 garlic cloves, peeled and chopped
200g/7oz spinach leaves

juice of ½ lemon
3 tbsp oat milk
1 tbsp nutritional yeast
⅛ tsp nutmeg
½ sea salt
4tbsp tahini

For the tomato sauce
3 tbsp olive oil
1 red onion, peeled and chopped
  (save the skin for dyeing)
3 garlic cloves, peeled and chopped
6 tomatoes, or 1 can chopped tomatoes
  (about 400g/14oz)
2 tbsp date molasses
1 tsp nutritional yeast
½ tsp sweet paprika
¼ tsp spicy paprika
½ tsp thyme
1 tsp sea salt flakes

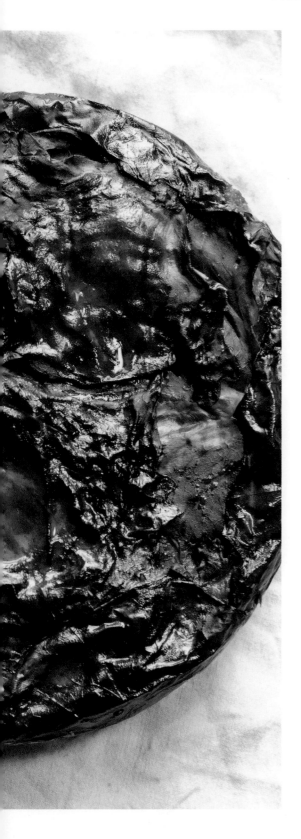

Method

01 Remove the cabbage cores with a sharp knife (save any discarded pieces for the dye), and soak the cabbages in a bowl of freshly boiled water for 8 minutes to ease the leaf-peeling process. Meanwhile, bring a large pan of water to the boil. Peel the largest leaves of each cabbage and submerge them in the boiling water. Cook for 10–15 minutes until the leaves are soft, drain, and set aside (save the cooking water for dyeing).

02 While the leaves are cooling, prepare the lentil ragù. In a saucepan, cover the lentils with water and bring to the boil. Cook for 15 minutes, or until the lentils are *al dente*, then drain. Heat the oil in a large frying pan and add the onions. Fry on a low heat for 5 minutes, or until soft. Add the garlic, leek, and mushrooms and cook for 4–6 minutes, until the mushrooms have softened and shrunken. Stir in the cooked lentils, Worcestershire sauce, spices, nutritional yeast, and salt. Cook on a gentle heat for 7 minutes. Remove from the heat and season to taste.

03 For the creamy greens, heat the oil in a medium frying pan. Lower the heat, add the onions, and cook for 5 minutes until soft. Add the garlic and cook for a further minute. Tip in the spinach, lemon juice, and oat milk, and cook until the leaves have wilted. Stir in the nutritional yeast, nutmeg, and salt, and remove from the heat. In a small bowl, whisk 4 tbsp of cold water with the tahini, and, once creamy, add to the spinach and mix to coat.

04 To make the tomato sauce, fry the onions in oil on a low heat for 5 minutes until soft. Add the garlic and cook for a further minute. Add the tomatoes, molasses, nutritional yeast, spices, and salt. Simmer for 10–15 minutes, or until the sauce has thickened, and set aside.

05 Heat the oven to 180°C/160°C fan/350°F/Gas 4. Grease a 35 x 25 x 7-cm/14 x 10 x 3-in roasting dish or a 23-cm/9-in springform baking tin. Cover the bottom (sides are optional) with cooked cabbage leaves, overlapping them to cover the surface completely. Add the ragù and cover with another layer of leaves. Repeat with the creamed greens, then with the tomato sauce and cover in a final layer of leaves.

06 Brush the top with olive oil and bake for 40 minutes or until the edges of the leaves start to brown. Cool for 10 minutes before serving.

Red Cabbage, Carrot, and Currant Slaw

Serves 4 as light main or 8 as a side

Out of the cabbage bunch, this is the least productive recipe in terms of generating dyestuff. While the other recipes leave you with nearly ready-made dye vats, this rather skimpily adds only what is necessary to remove from the cabbage, such as damaged outer leaves and the core, before you consume the rest of the cabbage raw. Still, I had to include this quick and healthy slaw – a favourite summer staple, and packed with a vibrancy in flavour that is utterly disproportionate to how incredibly easy it is to make. On a busy weekday, a bowl of this with some tahini dressing will fuel me with energy for the whole afternoon.

Ingredients

1 small red cabbage
1 red onion
4 carrots, coarsely grated
30g/1oz/¼ cup currants
40g/1½oz/¼ cup sunflower seeds
4 tbsp olive oil
2 tbsp balsamic vinegar
1 tsp sea salt
freshly ground black pepper

Method

01 Cut the cabbage into four wedges and remove the core
    (save it, alongside any discarded leaves, for dyeing).
    Chop the wedges finely; I like to cut mine to about
    3–4mm (⅛in) wide, rather than thin ribbons, to keep a
    bit of crunch.

02 Chop the onion proportionately to the cabbage (keep
    the skin for dying). Add both to a large bowl, alongside
    the rest of the ingredients, and mix well. Serve at room
    temperature, or refrigerate and serve cold.

Dye with *Cabbage*

I recently discovered that my neighbour in the next plot, Ulrike, is also interested in natural dye. It was a lovely surprise – Ulrike and I chat a lot, but mostly about the amount of rain, how to grow dahlias from cuttings, or the terrible slug problem this year. She's an amazing gardener, with a wild plot brimming with flowers and grasses, like a miniature meadow. "Impractical plants", she called them once, though she does grow many stunning vegetables, too. Ulrike is a senior lecturer in prehistoric archaeology, which is evident in her digging abilities, and in how much she knows about the history of plants and their cultural importance. It therefore made complete sense that her experiments with natural dyes are focused on their prehistoric uses trying to understand how they were used, and for what purposes. She told me that the most robust shades were generally extracted from plants that did not provide other benefits, such as madder. "Red cabbage surely wasn't a popular dye agent then?" "No," Ulrike laughed, but immediately confessed that, as an avid cabbage fan, she does dye yarn with its cooking water, despite it not being the most lasting dye.

A fugitive dye

This didn't surprise me. Even a quick boil extracts the most mesmerizing deep blue that would appeal to any creatively inclined eye. But cabbage is somewhat of a "fugitive dye" – not as fleeting as beetroot (which I was gutted not to include in this book for this very reason), but not as long-lasting as the four others I've explored here. For this reason I invest a little more effort in treating the fabric before I dye it, for maximum absorption. I always pre-bind it with plant-based milk, and mordant it in a separate dye vat to my main cabbage vat (pp20–21). I also try to choose different fabrics as a base for my cabbage shorts: light, speckled, beige French linen I bought on a small roll at an antique market; a rather wrecked old stripy linen tablecloth; a pair of second-hand gingham cotton curtains. These cloths have their own character that will come more to the fore when the initially strong shade fades to a (delightful) blueish-grey – although I may very well choose to dye it again and again over time.

Ironically, the reason cabbage isn't as "washfast" (p19) as the other natural dyes we explore is also what makes it one of the most alluring. As you may recall from some hands-on chemistry lessons, red cabbage is a universal pH indicator due to its natural anthocyanin, a water-soluble pigment that changes colour when mixed with an acid or a base. In more acidic environments it reddens, while more alkaline solutions bring it closer to a bluish-green shade. As a dyer, it is an exciting prism to play with, but it's far from an exact science. Much as in cooking, the outcome depends on so many variants that have nothing to do with how closely you follow the recipe. Here, it could be the acidity level of the soil the cabbage grew in, the natural pH level of the water on that given day, how clean the dye vat I'm using is, and what I cleaned it with.

For the same reason, washing your cabbage shorts can yield unexpected results, as it may dramatically intervene with the pH level. Even so, here is a rough guide to the colours I've extracted from cabbage using different mordants and solutions. I'm confident that after a while, you would be able to add your own to the list.

Blues and purples

Most of the shades you could extract from the red cabbage sit on this spectrum. The most simple ones are the ice-blues and lilacs you will get from simply simmering the fabric in the cabbage cooking water, the exact shade depending mainly on the water's pH level. If your water takes you towards blue, adding bicarbonate of soda gradually will make light shades of cornflower or sweet powder blue and even dusty turquoise (the only shade of this colour I could personally stomach). Adding acidic solutions, such as vinegar (different types vary the shades) and cream of tartar, will take the fabric towards shades of deep purple such as royal ruby, amethyst purple, and, in very high amounts, to bright shades between violet and magenta.

Greys

These are achieved by introducing iron mordant to the main dye vat, making the dye a lot more wash-and lightfast. A modest addition will result in a lovely bluish sleet, while a hefty amount will change it more towards light steel. You could also add iron to any of the pH experiments described previously to make the colours more sombre. Another "cocktail" that yields a powerful deep grey mixes the cabbage leaves with oak galls or acorns shells – oak trees are a fascinatingly diverse dye source in their own right.

Earthy hues

These are perhaps some of my favourite hues, and ones you don't need a recipe for, as if you head to p192 and enjoy the Cabbage Oysters, the reserved stock from the recipe can be used as a dye to make rich, earthy shades. To strengthen their melancholic character, add 2–5 more tea bags to the vat, or some iron mordant. The results from making these more earthy hues will be much longer-lasting than your standard cabbage dye.

See pages 18–23 for more detailed information on techniques, dyestuff, mordants, and dye vat ratios.

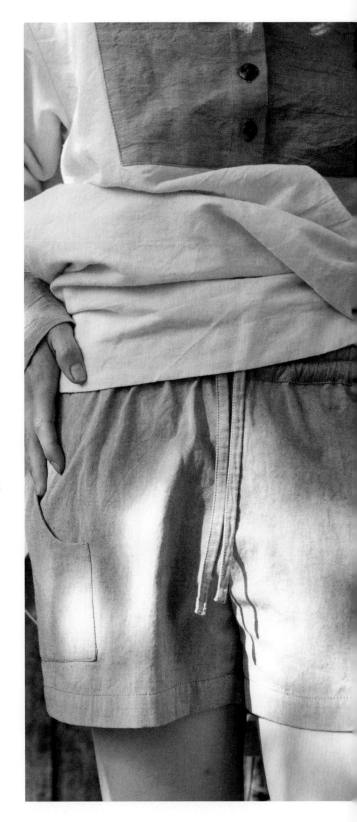

Cabbage colour range

The Cabbage Shorts are typically 100–200g (3½oz–7oz), depending on your fabric and elastic of choice. These tentative dye "recipes" are for 100g (3½oz) of fabric – multiply the quantities as required and use enough water to cover the fabric. Bear in mind that the shade may vary depending on your fabric, water and soil pH level, the quality of your modifiers, and serendipity.

Sleet grey

Medium-weight French linen, bound with oat milk and mordanted with alum. Dyed with the cooking water of 100g (3½oz) cabbage, 1 tbsp of iron-infused water, and 1 tbsp of iron sulphate for every 100g (3½oz) of fabric. Boiled and simmered for 2 hours, steeped for 6 hours.

Icey blue

Lightweight French linen tablecloth, bound with oat milk and mordanted with alum. Dyed with the cooking water of 100g (3½oz) cabbage, 1½ tsp of bicarbonate of soda, for 100g (3½oz) of fabric. Boiled and simmered for 2 hours, steeped for overnight.

Dusty cornflower

Medium-weight antique coarse linen, bound with oat milk and mordanted with alum. Dyed with the cooking water of 120g (4oz) cabbage, 1 tbsp of bicarbonate of soda, and 1 tsp of iron-infused water for every 100g (3½oz) of fabric. Boiled and simmered for 3 hours, steeped for overnight.

Rosy tan

Medium-weight French linen bound with oat milk and mordanted with alum. 100g (3½oz) of fabric were dyed using the cooking water from the Cabbage Oysters (pp192–193). Boiled and simmered for 2 hours, steeped for 12 hours.

Perky mauve

Medium-weight coarse antique linen, bound with oat milk and mordanted with alum. Dyed with the cooking water of 80g (2¾oz) cabbage and 1 tbsp of cream of tartar for every 100g (3½oz) of fabric. Boiled and simmered for 2 hours, steeped for 4 hours.

Cool grey

Medium-weight antique linen, bound with oat milk and mordanted with alum. Dyed with the cooking water of 80g (2¾oz) cabbage and 1 tsp of iron-infused water for every 100g (3½oz) of fabric. Boiled and simmered for 2 hours, steeped for 6 hours.

Charcoal grey

Medium-weight antique linen, bound with oat milk and mordanted with alum. Dyed with the cooking water of 100g (3½oz) cabbage, 1 tbsp of iron-infused water, and 1 tbsp of dried acorn shells and oak galls mix for every 100g (3½oz) of fabric. Boiled and simmered for 2 hours, steeped for 6 hours.

The Cabbage Shorts

When it's warm enough for me to wear the Cabbage Shorts, I know I'll pretty much live in them: their relaxed fit and elasticated waistband make them ideal attire for a long day at the allotment – and they are even comfortable enough to sleep in. Yet their unusual pocket detail and rather sophisticated array of colours make them work, too, for a more "dressed up" summer evening look, combined with a crisp white button-down shirt and some high-heeled clogs.

Construction

Shown on the right are the pattern pieces for the Cabbage Shorts (please see Pattern Sheets 1 and 4).

You will also need soft elastic for the waistband, 4cm (1½in) wide. Check the length of your elastic by stretching it around your body, roughly 7cm (2½in) below your natural waist. Pull until the elastic feels snug, but not tight. Add 4cm (1½in) for seam allowance.

All seam allowances are 1cm (⅜in) unless otherwise stated.

Measurements

Please refer to the appendix on p222 for size charts and fabric requirements. Determine your size according to your waist and hip measurements.

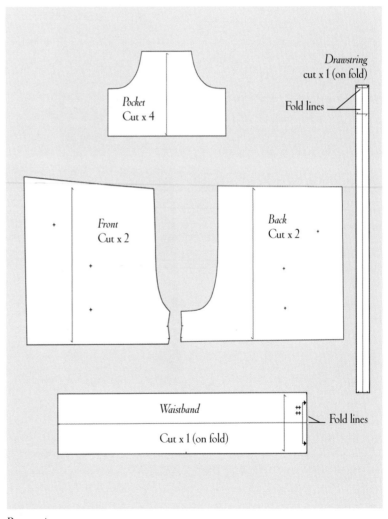

Pattern pieces

01

Keep notches shorter than 7mm (¼in), so they don't cut into the seam.

Topstitch 1cm (⅜in) away from the edge.

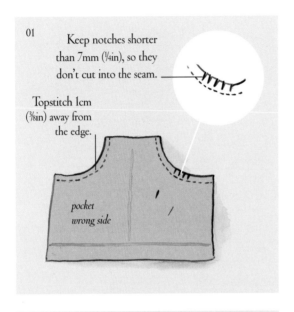

*pocket
wrong side*

02

Make sure the pocket layers are perfectly aligned.

inner pocket

Fold and press the top, sides, and bottom edges towards the inner pocket by 1cm (⅜in).

03

Sew 1cm (⅜in) away from the edge.

*outside leg
seam*

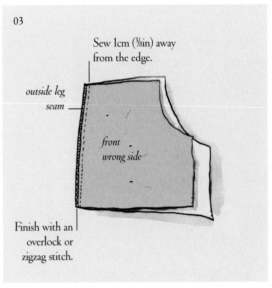

*front
wrong side*

Finish with an overlock or zigzag stitch.

01 **Prepare the pockets**

These patch pockets open from both sides rather than from the top and are each cut in two layers to strengthen their curved opening line. Pin one pair of pocket pieces right sides together. Stitch the curved lines on both sides, 1cm (⅜in) away from the edge. Cut notches into the roundest part of the seam allowance to achieve a smoother curve.

02 Press the seam allowances open. Turn right side out. Decide which side will be visible from the front (the outer pocket) and which will line the inside of the pocket (the inner pocket). Fold and press the top, side, and bottom edges towards the inner pocket by 1cm (⅜in). Repeat steps 1–2 for the other pocket.

03 **Sew the side seam**

Take one set of front and back pieces and, with right sides together, pin and sew the outside leg seam. Overlock or zigzag stitch the seam allowances together and press towards the back. Repeat with the other set of front and back pieces.

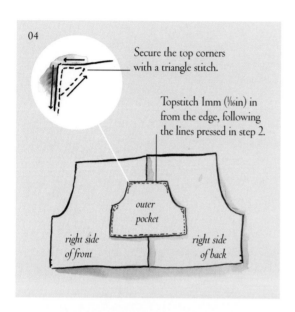

04

Secure the top corners
with a triangle stitch.

Topstitch 1mm (¹⁄₁₆in) in
from the edge, following
the lines pressed in step 2.

*outer
pocket*

*right side
of front*

*right side
of back*

04 Attach the pockets

Open up one of the assembled front-and-back pieces
and lay it right side up. Pin a patch pocket according to
the markings on the pattern. Topstitch around the
straight sides 1mm (¹⁄₁₆in) in from the edge. For
longevity, secure the top corners with a triangle stitch
(see step 3, p91). Press. Repeat for the other assembled
front-and-back piece.

05 Press the hem

You will sew the hem in place only after you stitch the
inner leg seam. However, it is easier to press a crisp
hemline when you can still lay the assembled front-and-
back pieces flat. Fold and press the hem to the wrong
side by 1cm (⅜in) (a), and then by by 2.5cm (1in) (b).
Repeat for the other assembled front-and-back piece.

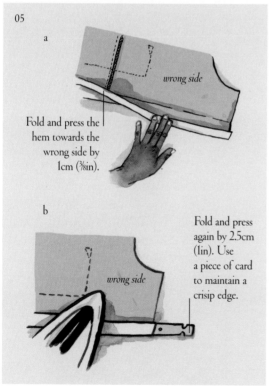

05

a

wrong side

Fold and press the
hem towards the
wrong side by
1cm (⅜in).

b

wrong side

Fold and press
again by 2.5cm
(1in). Use
a piece of card
to maintain a
crisip edge.

Cabbage Bermudas

As with many of the garments in this book, you can
adapt the pattern. For a longer, Bermuda-length
variation, add about 38cm (15in) to the hemline.

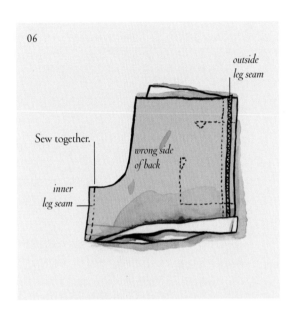

06

Sew together.

inner
leg seam

outside
leg seam

*wrong side
of back*

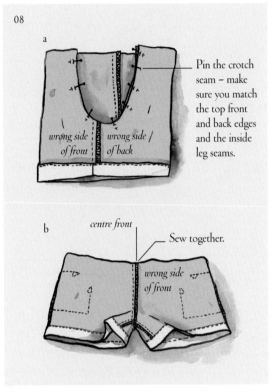

08

a

Pin the crotch
seam – make
sure you match
the top front
and back edges
and the inside
leg seams.

*wrong side
of front*   *wrong side
of back*

b

centre front

Sew together.

*wrong side
of front*

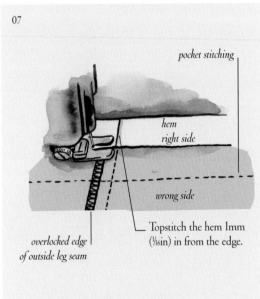

07

pocket stitching

*hem
right side*

wrong side

Topstitch the hem 1mm
(⅟₁₆in) in from the edge.

*overlocked edge
of outside leg seam*

06 **Sew the inner-leg seam**

With the right sides together, pin and stitch the inside
leg seam. Overlock or zigzag stitch the seam allowances
together and press towards the back. Repeat for the
other side to complete the other leg.

07 **Sew the hem**

Press the hem fold back in place and topstitch 1mm
(⅟₁₆in) in from the folded edge. Press. Repeat for the
other leg.

08 **Sew the crotch seam**

With the right sides together, matching the top front and
back edges and the inside leg seams, pin the crotch seam,
which forms the centre front and back of the shorts (a).
Sew together, working from the back waist through the
crotch and up to the front waist. Overlock or zigzag stitch
the seam allowances together and press towards the right
front (b).

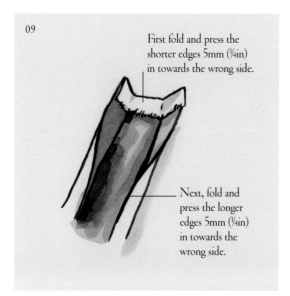

09

First fold and press the shorter edges 5mm (¼in) in towards the wrong side.

Next, fold and press the longer edges 5mm (¼in) in towards the wrong side.

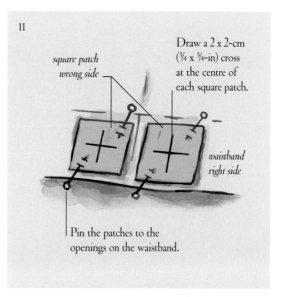

11

square patch wrong side

Draw a 2 x 2-cm (¾ x ¾-in) cross at the centre of each square patch.

waistband right side

Pin the patches to the openings on the waistband.

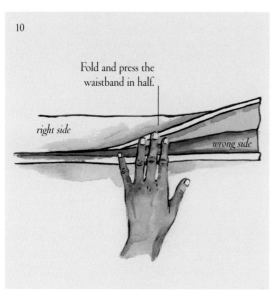

10

Fold and press the waistband in half.

right side

wrong side

09 **Sew the drawstring**

Fold and press the short edges to the wrong side by 5mm (¼in), then repeat with the long edges. Fold and press the drawstring in half, right side out. Topstitch 1mm (¹⁄₁₆in) away from the edge.

10 **Prepare the waistband**

Fold and press the long edges to the wrong side by 1cm (⅜in). Fold and press the waistband in half, wrong sides together.

11 Referring to the markings on the pattern for position, pin small patches, each around 3 x 3cm (³⁄₁₆ x ³⁄₁₆in), to the right side of the fabric. Draw a 2 x 2-cm (¾ x ¾-in) cross in the centre of each patch; if you prefer buttonholes or eyelets, apply small patches of interfacing to the wrong side of the fabric).

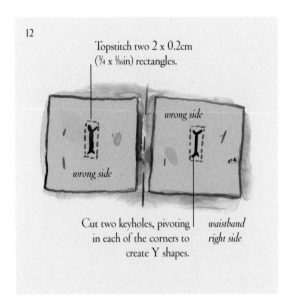

12

Topstitch two 2 x 0.2cm
(¾ x ¹⁄₁₆in) rectangles.

wrong side

wrong side

Cut two keyholes, pivoting
in each of the corners to
create Y shapes.

*waistband
right side*

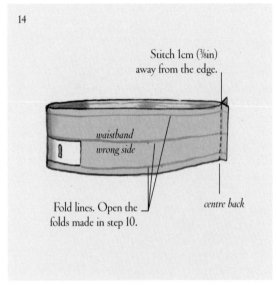

14

Stitch 1cm (³⁄₈in)
away from the edge.

*waistband
wrong side*

Fold lines. Open the
folds made in step 10.

centre back

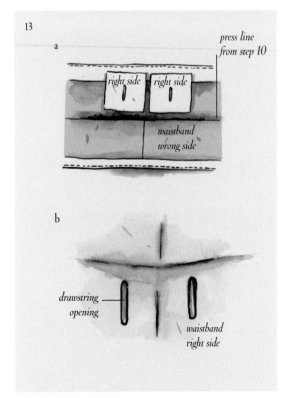

13

a

*press line
from step 10*

right side   *right side*

*waistband
wrong side*

b

*drawstring
opening*

*waistband
right side*

12 Topstitch two 2cm x 2mm (¾ x ¹⁄₁₆in) rectangles. Cut a
keyhole in the middle of each rectangle, pivoting
towards each of the corners carefully, creating
double-ended Y-shapes.

13 Turn the square patches through the keyholes to the
wrong side of the waistband (a) to create the openings
for the drawstring (b). Press.

14 Pin the short ends of the waistband right sides together
and stitch. Press the seam open. This seam is the centre
back of the waistband.

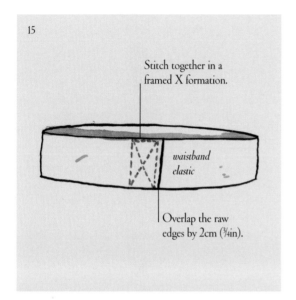

15

Stitch together in a framed X formation.

waistband elastic

Overlap the raw edges by 2cm (¾in).

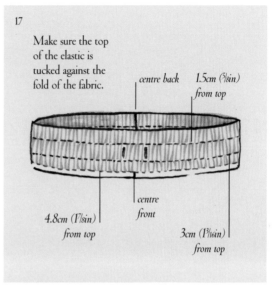

17

Make sure the top of the elastic is tucked against the fold of the fabric.

centre back

1.5cm (⅝in) from top

centre front

4.8cm (1⅞in) from top

3cm (1³⁄₁₆in) from top

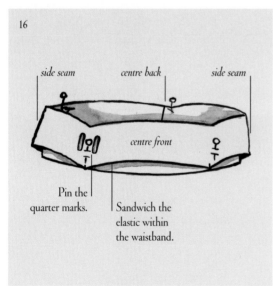

16

side seam

centre back

side seam

centre front

Pin the quarter marks.

Sandwich the elastic within the waistband.

15 **Sew the elastic**
Overlap the raw ends of the waistband elastic by 2cm (¾in) and stitch them together in a framed X formation. Repeat the stitch for added strength. Once sewn, using the seam as the centre back, mark the centre front and back and use these marks to divide the elastic into quarters.

16 **Sandwich the elastic within the waistband**
Pin the quarter marks to the centre back, centre front, and side seams of the waistband.

17 **Sew the elastic to the waistband**
Start at the centre back. Sew a row of stitching 1.5cm (⅝in) in from the top fold of the waistband. Hold on to the centre back with one hand, using your other hand to hold on to the side seam as you feed the fabric through, stretching the elastic as needed. Stitch around the entire waistband with the elastic stretched out and the fabric pulled taut, working by quarters to ensure even distribution. Using the same method, sew a second line of stitching 3cm (1¼in) in from the top fold and a third line 4.8cm (1⅞in) in from the top fold.

18

Pin in place
the front, sides
and back. Sew. *centre*
front

inner
waistband

front
right side

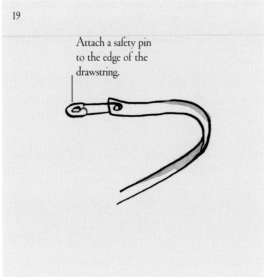

19

Attach a safety pin
to the edge of the
drawstring.

18 **Sew the waistband to the shorts**

Place the waistband against the shorts, right sides
together, aligning the raw edges. Pin the centre front
mark on the waistband to the centre front seam, the side
marks to the side seams, and the centre back mark to
the centre back seam. Make sure the drawstring
openings are at the centre front. Stretch out the
waistband between the pinned quarters until it sits flat
against the shorts. Starting at the centre back, stitch all
around – keep the fabric pulled taut, as in step 17, using
the bottom stitch line on the waistband as a guide.
Overlock or zigzag stitch the seam allowances together,
stretching the waistband in the same manner. Press the
seam towards the legs. Press the shorts all over.

19 **Insert the drawstring**

Attach a safety pin to the end of the drawstring and
feed it through the channel in the waistband, inserting
it through one opening and bringing it out through
the other.

Appendix

To choose your size, find your measurements in the Body Measurements table. It is common for these measurements to differ slightly from your body measurements, as the side seams of the patterns were laid out to allow you to grade in-between sizes easily. If you aren't sure, measure a similar garment that fits you well and compare these measurements to the Finished Garment Measurements.

The Fabric Requirements indicate the length required depending on your size and fabric width – this may be less predictable when upcycling textiles.

Onion dress

BODY MEASUREMENTS:

Measurement/size	8-12	14-16	18-20	22-24
Chest/bust	84–94cm/ 33–37in	94–104cm/ 37–41in	104–114cm/ 41–45in	114–124cm/ 45–49in
Waist	64–74cm/ 25¼–29¼in	74–82cm/ 29¼–32¼in	82–94cm/ 32¼–37in	94–104cm/ 37–41in

FINISHED GARMENT MEASUREMENTS:

Measurement/size	8-12	14-16	18-20	22-24
Chest/bust	146cm/57½in	151cm/59½in	156cm/61½in	161cm/63½in
Waist	160cm/63in	165cm/65in	170cm/67in	175cm/69in
Hem	181cm/71¼in	186cm/73¼in	191cm/75½in	196cm/77in
Length	84.5cm/33¼in	87cm/34¼in	88cm/34¼in	89cm/35in

FABRIC REQUIREMENTS:

Fabric width/size	8-12	14-16	18-20	22-24
120cm/48in	300cm/3⅜ yards	310cm/3⅜ yards	310cm/3⅜ yards	320cm/3½ yards
150cm/60in	275cm/3 yards	280cm/3 yards	280cm/3 yards	285cm/3⅛ yards
170cm/66in	240cm/2⅝ yards	245cm/2¾ yards	245cm/2¾ yards	250cm/2¾ yards
180cm/70in	240cm/2⅝ yards	245cm/2¾ yards	245cm/2¾ yards	250cm/2¾ yards
200cm/78in	210cm/2⅜ yards	220cm/2½ yards	225cm/2½ yards	230cm/2½ yards

Nettle duster

BODY MEASUREMENTS:

Measurement/size	6-8	10-12	14-16	18-20	22-24
Neck	35–37cm/ 13¾–14½in	37–38cm/ 14½–15in	38–39cm/ 15–15¼in	39–40cm/ 15¼–15¾in	40–42cm/ 15¾–16½in
Chest/bust	84–90cm/ 33–35½in	90–96cm/ 35½–37¾in	96–102cm/ 37¾–40in	102–110cm/ 40–43¼in	110–116cm/ 43¼–45½in
Waist	64–70cm/ 25¼–27½in	70–76cm/ 27½–30in	76–84cm/ 30–33in	84–94cm/ 33–37in	92–104cm/ 37–41in
Hip	88–94cm/ 34½–37in	94–100cm/ 37–39½in	100–106cm/ 39½–41¾in	106–114cm/ 41¾–45in	114–124cm/ 45–49in

FINISHED GARMENT MEASUREMENTS:

Measurement/size	6-8	10-12	14-16	18-20	22-24
Chest/bust	109cm/43in	114cm/45in	119cm/47in	124cm/49in	129cm/51in
Waist	106cm/41¾in	111cm/43¾in	116cm/45¾in	121cm/47¾in	126cm/49¾in
Hip	111cm/43¾in	116cm/45¾in	121cm/47¾in	126cm/49¾in	131cm/51¾in
Sleeve length	57.5cm/22½in	58.5cm/23in	59.5cm/23½in	61cm/24in	71cm/28in
Shoulder	17cm/6½in	17.5cm/6¾in	18cm/7in	18.5cm/7¼in	19.5cm/7¾in
Length	101.5cm/40in	103cm/40½in	104cm/41in	105.5cm/41½in	106.5cm/42in
Hem	116cm/45¾in	121cm/47¾in	126cm/49¾in	131cm/51¾in	135cm/53¾in

FABRIC REQUIREMENTS:

Fabric width/size	6-8	10-12	14-16	18-20	22-24
120cm/48in	260cm/2⅞ yards	265cm/2⅞ yards	270cm/3 yards	280cm/3⅛ yards	285cm/3⅛ yards
150cm/60in	220cm/2½ yards	220cm/2½ yards	225cm/2½ yards	225cm/2½ yards	240cm/2⅝ yards
170cm/66in	180cm/2 yards	185cm/2 yards	185cm/2 yards	220cm/2½ yards	225cm/2½ yards
180cm/70in	175cm/1⅞ yards	180cm/2 yards	185cm/2 yards	180cm/2 yards	215cm/2⅜ yards
200cm/78in	165cm/1⅞ yards	165cm/1⅞ yards	170cm/1⅞ yards	180cm/2 yards	180cm/2 yards

Rhubarb bolero

BODY MEASUREMENTS:

Measurement/size	8-10	12-14	16-18	20-22
Chest/bust	84–92cm/ 33–36¼in	92–98cm/ 36¼–38½in	98–108cm/ 38½–42½in	108–116cm/ 42½–45¾in
Waist	64–74cm/ 25–29in	74–82cm/ 29–32¼in	82–90cm/ 32¼in–35½in	90–98cm/ 35½in–38½in

FINISHED GARMENT MEASUREMENTS:

Measurement/size	8-10	12-14	16-18	20-22
Chest/bust	96cm/37¾in	101cm/39¾in	105.5cm/41½in	110.5cm/43½in
Waist	89cm/35in	94cm/37in	98.5cm/38¾in	104cm/41in
Neck to sleeve hem	22.5cm/8¾in	24cm/9½in	25.5cm/10in	27cm/10½in
Sleeve opening	42.5cm/16¾in	45cm/17¾in	47.5cm/18¾in	49.5cm/19½in
Length	38.5cm/15in	40cm/15¾in	41cm/16in	42.5cm/16¾in

FABRIC REQUIREMENTS:

Fabric width/size	8-10	12-14	16-18	20-22
120cm/48in	95cm/1⅛ yards	100cm/1⅛ yards	105cm/1¼ yards	110cm/1¼ yards
150cm/60in	75cm/⅞ yard	75cm/⅞ yard	80cm/⅞ yard	80cm/⅞ yard
170cm/66in	75cm/⅞ yard	75cm/⅞ yard	80cm/⅞ yard	80cm/⅞ yard
180cm/70in	70cm/¾ yard	75cm/¾ yard	75cm/¾ yard	75cm/¾ yard
200cm/78in	55cm/⅝ yard	60cm/¾ yard	60cm/¾ yard	60cm/¾ yard

Blackberry shirt(dress)

BODY MEASUREMENTS:

Measurement/size	6-8	10-12	14-16	18-20	22-24
Neck	35–37cm/13¾–14½in	37–38cm/14½–15in	38–39cm/15–15¼in	39–40cm/15¼–15¾in	40–42cm/15¾–16½in
Chest/bust	84–90cm/33–35½in	90–96cm/35½–37¾in	96–102cm/37¾–40in	102–110cm/40–43¼in	110–116cm/43¼–45½in
Waist	64–70cm/25¼–27½in	70–76cm/27½in–30in	76–84cm/30–33in	84–94cm/33–37in	92–104cm/37–41in
Hip	88–94cm/34½–37in	94–100cm/37–40in	100–106cm/40–41¾in	106–114cm/41¾–45in	114–154cm/45–48¾in

FINISHED GARMENT MEASUREMENTS:

Measurement/size	6-8	10-12	14-16	18-20	22-24
Collar (buttoned)	49.5cm/19½in	52cm/20½in	54.5cm/21½in	57cm/22½in	59.5cm/23½in
Chest/bust	99cm/39in	109cm/43in	119cm/47in	129cm/51in	139cm/55in
Waist	94.5cm/37in	104.5cm/41in	114.5cm/45in	124.5cm/49in	134.5cm/53in
Hip	97cm/38in	107cm/42in	117cm/46in	127cm/50in	137cm/54in
Shoulder	11.5cm/4½in	12cm/4¾in	12.5cm/5in	13.5cm/5¼in	14cm/5½in
Sleeve length	60cm/23½in	61.5cm/24¼in	62.5cm/24¾in	63.5cm/25in	65m/25½24in
Cuff	22.5cm/9in	24cm/9½in	25cm/10in	26.5cm/10½in	27.5cm/11in
Front length – top shoulder to hem (dress)	96.5cm/38in	98cm/38½in	99.5cm/39in	101.5cm/40in	102cm/40¼in
Back length – top yoke to hem (dress)	98.5cm/38¾in	99.5cm/39¼in	101cm/39¾in	102cm/40¼in	103cm/40½in
Front length – top shoulder to hem (shirt)	67cm/26¼in	68cm/26¾in	69.5cm/27¼in	70.5cm/27¾in	71.5cm/28¼in
Back length – top yoke to hem (shirt)	64cm/25in	65.5cm/25½in	66.5cm/26in	68cm/26¾in	69cm/27in

FABRIC REQUIREMENTS:

Fabric width/size	6-8	10-12	14-16	18-20	22-24
120cm/48in	270cm/3 yards	275cm/3 yards	280cm/3 yards	285cm/3⅛ yards	290cm/3¼ yards
150cm/60in	195cm/2⅛ yards	200cm/2¼ yards	220cm/2½ yards	225cm/2½ yards	230cm/2½ yards
170cm/66in	185cm/2 yards	185cm/2 yards	190cm/2 yards	190cm/2 yards	200cm/2.2 yards
180cm/70in	160cm/1¾ yards	165cm/1⅞ yards	165cm/1⅞ yards	185cm/2 yards	185cm/2 yards
200cm/78in	150cm/1¾ yards	160cm/1¾ yards	165cm/1⅞ yards	170cm/1⅞yards	170cm/1⅞ yards

Cabbage shorts

BODY MEASUREMENTS:

Measurement /size	8	10	12	14	16	18	20	22
Waist	64–66cm/ 25¼–26in	66–72cm/ 26–28¼in	72–76cm/ 28¼–30in	76–80cm/ 30–31½in	80–84cm/ 31½–33in	84–88cm/ 33–34½	88–94cm/ 34.5–37in	94–98cm/ 37–38½in
Hip	84–88cm/ 33–34½in	88–92cm/ 34½–36¼in	92–96cm/ 36¼–37¾in	96–100cm/ 37¾–39½in	100–106cm/ 39½–41¾in	106–110cm/ 41¾–43¼in	110–114cm/ 43¼–45in	114–120cm/ 45–47¼in

FINISHED GARMENT MEASUREMENTS:

Measurement /size	8	10	12	14	16	18	20	22
Waistband (fully stretched)	97cm/ 38¼in	100cm/ 39½in	103cm/ 40½in	106cm/ 41½in	109cm/ 43in	112cm/ 44in	115cm/ 45¼in	118cm/ 46½in
Hips	106cm/ 41½in	111cm/ 43¾in	116cm/ 45½in	120cm/ 47¼in	125cm/ 49¼in	130cm/ 51¼in	135cm/ 53¼in	140cm/ 55in
Thigh	54.5cm/ 21½in	57cm/ 22½in	59.5cm/ 23½in	62cm/ 24½in	64cm/ 25¼in	66.5cm/ 26in	69cm/ 27in	71.5cm/ 28in
Length	37.5cm/ 14¾in	38cm/ 15in	38.5cm/ 15¼in	39cm/ 15½in	39.5cm/ 15½in	40.5cm/ 16in	41cm/ 16¼in	41.5cm/ 16½in

FABRIC REQUIREMENTS:

Fabric width /size	8	10	12	14	16	18	20	22
120cm/48in	115cm/ 1¼ yards	120cm/ 1⅜ yards	120cm/ 1⅜ yards	125cm/ 1⅜ yards	150cm/ 1¾ yards	155cm/ 1¾ yards	155cm/ 1¾ yards	155cm/ 1¾ yards
150cm/60in	90cm/ 1 yard	95cm/ 1 yard	100cm/ 1⅛ yards	110cm/ 1⅛ yards	125cm/ 1⅜ yards	130cm/ 1½ yards	130cm/ 1½ yards	135cm/ 1½ yards
170cm/66in	70cm/ ¾ yard	70cm/ ¾ yard	75cm/ ⅞ yard	80cm/ ⅞ yard	80cm/ ⅞ yard	80cm/ ⅞ yard	85cm/ 1 yard	85cm/ 1 yard
180cm/70in	65cm/ ¾ yard	70cm/ ¾ yard	75cm/ ⅞ yard	75cm/ ⅞ yard	75cm/ ⅞ yard	80cm/ ⅞ yard	80cm/ ⅞ yard	80cm/ ⅞ yard
200cm/78in	60cm/ ¾ yard	65cm/ ¾ yard	65cm/ ¾ yard	65cm/ ¾ yard	70cm/ ¾ yard	75cm/ ⅞ yard	80cm/ ⅞ yard	80cm/ ⅞ yard